How to Give Yourself a Hand Back Up

Resilience skills for emotional and relationship success

Dr Richard Bolstad

How to Give Yourself a Hand Back Up

Resilience, the ability to prepare for, survive and evolve through challenges, depends on a series of skills and actions that can be learned. Dr Richard Bolstad is a qualified teacher, nurse, psychotherapist, and NLP Trainer. He teaches Resilience and trains Trainers to teach it across the planet, in businesses, for emergency first responders, and at the scene of major crises such as wars, earthquakes and climate disasters. You can contact him at www.transformations.net.nz

TRANSFORMING
COMMUNICATION

How to Give Yourself a Hand Back Up

Contents

Preface:

In this book, I aim to bring together, as I do on my Resilience trainings around the world, three fields. One is the Psychology of Resilience, summarised in the quote below from the APA. Another is the neuroscience of resilience as revealed in ongoing research over the last twenty years. The third is the field of NLP, which offers a rather extraordinary rethinking of how we deal with challenges to resilience such as PTSD. In the last few years well replicated controlled experiments have demonstrated the effectiveness in particular of the NLP intervention for Reconsolidation of Traumatic Memories. This intervention, in hundreds of studied cases, has better than 90% effectiveness in swiftly and permanently removing the distressing experience of PTSD, and that in itself teaches us some extremely important understandings about how resilience works and why it may have failed in the past.

Those new to the research on resilience may be surprised that I include so much in this book about creating loving relationships. The APA make it clear in their description on the next page that this is simply the number one thing you would want to set up to provide yourself resilience. I understand, of course, that many people will have picked up this book because they want to find a way individually to become more resilient. You sure will learn that here too. But the title "How to Give Yourself a Hand Back Up" is purposefully ambiguous. Giving yourself a hand also involves working out how to create external supports, and that involves a paradox we sometimes forget in our modern society. One of the best ways to become more independent is to know when you need support from others and use it. Enjoy the journey back to happiness!

Factors in Resilience
American Psychological Association
(https://www.apa.org/helpcenter/road-resilience)

A combination of factors contributes to resilience. Many studies show that the primary factor in resilience is having caring and supportive relationships within and outside the family. Relationships that create love and trust, provide role models and offer encouragement and reassurance help bolster a person's resilience.

Several additional factors are associated with resilience, including:

- The capacity to make realistic plans and take steps to carry them out.
- A positive view of yourself and confidence in your strengths and abilities.
- Skills in communication and problem solving.
- The capacity to manage strong feelings and impulses.

All of these [additional capacities] are factors that people can develop in themselves.

Chapter 1:
Finding Happiness In A Challenging World

The Story of Milton Erickson

Sometimes life is tougher than we expect. It's amazing that you've survived this far, and life has not finished with you yet, by the way. But some people seem to thrive on the challenges of life, and others feel like they are being worn down. The difference is what psychologists have come to call resilience. Resilience doesn't just mean bouncing back after a challenge knocks you down: it means actually coming out of these kind of experiences with an enriched sense of what life is about and of who you are. Sound too good to be true? Let me tell you more.

Of all the hundreds of stories I tell when I am running Resilience training around the world, none is more memorable to my students than the life story of one person who created so many of the skills I teach: a remarkable medical doctor called Milton Erickson. While I never personally met Milton, at least six of my own direct teachers were his students and told his story with such passion that I feel as if I was there with them. Now, I want to take you into his life story too.

Erickson was born in 1901 in a log cabin in Wisconsin, USA. As a child he was diagnosed with several sensory problems including a severe form of colour blindness where he could only see the colour purple, an inability to detect tonal differences in sounds, and a dyslexia that made it hard for him to identify the orientation and direction of written letters. At the age of 17 he was physically paralysed by the viral infection polio, and almost died.

Trapped in his wheelchair all day, he could have just given up. But Erickson had the prior experience of colour blindness, tone deafness and dyslexia, and he was accustomed to paying attention more carefully than most. He noticed that his body responded physically to his remembering of activities such as walking. By recreating these memories he gradually activated his own muscles and retrained his body to walk. It took two years, and man did Erickson push himself, setting ever more difficult tasks. And through all that he learned more about his body than most people learn in a lifetime. People used to ask him "How did you achieve so much?". Erickson's answer was unsettling. He would say "Well see; I was lucky. I had polio."

Erickson graduated from the University of Wisconsin in 1928, as a psychologist and medical practitioner, and after an extraordinary career as a Psychiatrist, ultimately became Clinical Director of the Arizona State

Hospital in 1948. Only a few years later, he was stricken by post-polio syndrome, a resurgence of symptoms which required him to move back to a wheelchair. Even from this challenge, he managed to recreate a life where he was able to inspire and assist so many other human beings. In his retirement he continued to train thousands in his method of working with people who had psychiatric problems; a method which emerged from both his own experience and from his training in hypnotherapy. He called his method "utilization", by which he meant that he utilised whatever skills, experiences, responses and attitudes each individual person had already, rather than imposing one predesigned model of therapy on everyone. One assumption behind utilisation is that everyone has a different way of interpreting the world, and if you want to help them change, their new ways of behaving have to make sense in that way of interpreting things, at least at the start. That flexibility of approach makes it extremely difficult to copy Erickson's way of working, though many have since attempted to "model" or copy his specific verbal and non-verbal techniques.

It is impossible to overstate the profound effect that Milton Erickson has had on the way we understand "psychotherapy", "coaching" and all human change. His daughters Betty Anne and Roxanne, in their book written with Dan Short, explain that the hidden key to his success as a therapist was the way he lived his own life: "Erickson's life was characterized by determination, resiliency, and hope. The ideas that he advocated within his therapy are the same ideas exemplified by how he lived his life. He had a profound appreciation for the strength that comes from a willingness to establish meaningful objectives and then doing something in relation to that goal. For Erickson, progress was not dependent on things going "his way."" (Short, Erickson and Erickson-Klein, 2005, Kindle Locations 317-319).

NLP

In 1975, Linguistics experts John Grinder and Richard Bandler wrote a book analysing the linguistic patterns with which Erickson spoke. They hoped to use their knowledge of word use to understand how he had his remarkable effect. Erickson noted "Although this book by Richard Bandler and John Grinder, to which I am contributing this Preface, is far from being a complete description of my methodologies, as they so clearly state it is a much better explanation of how I work than I, myself, can give." He referred perhaps to the fact that they kind of understood what he was doing, but not really "why" he was doing it. Their naming of their own work as "Neurolinguistic Programming" (NLP) betrays their focus on the technical "coding" of his work rather than the choices he was making in the background. I hope I pay more attention here to the "attitudes" behind Milton's work, AND I am aware that this little book is also not a complete description of his work.

The biggest challenge we face as human beings is perhaps that we arrive with batteries included, but without a users' manual! NLP's precise understanding of the way the brain works can be compared to a computer "User's Manual". Without the manual, you know that the computer has a vast memory and can do amazing things. If you play around with it eventually you'll manage to stumble on some of those things. But with the manual, you can choose exactly what you want to do, and have the computer do it perfectly every time. In NLP, we know the programs (or "strategies" to use the NLP term) which naturally excellent communicators have accidentally stumbled on: the strategy for setting goals so they have a high chance of becoming realities, the strategy for bouncing back from the inevitable challenges of life, the strategy for creating loving relationships that last through time ….

Secondly, though, human beings are more than programmable computers. Resilience is not just the ability to set and achieve goals, it is the ability to find those activities meaningful and joyful, even when things do not go the way you wanted. And loving relationships, key factors in doing that, are the result not just of a "communication strategy", but of an openness of heart that cannot be faked.

The Core Beliefs Shared by Resilient People

The skills you are learning are based on a set of key ideas, and even in the methodical thinking of NLP, these key ideas were described as "presuppositions of NLP". While we do not claim these ideas are "true", we do think they are *useful*. To understand this difference, imagine two people, Sharon and Joan. Joan has the idea that people are basically friendly, and Sharon has the idea that people are basically unfriendly. They both go out to the same party. We can be sure that they will get different results. NLP would say that Joan probably has a more *useful* idea for using at a party. That idea might not be "true". But even if it was not true (even if people could be proved to be mainly unfriendly) Joan's idea might still be more useful. To get better results, you don't have to *believe* these ideas, you only need to "act as if they were true".

1. Our Internal Maps Of The World Are Not The Same As The Actual Territory Outside And Each Of Us Has Our Own Unique Maps

In any large city there are at least two different kinds of map: road maps and subway maps. Neither map is more "real" than the other, but they are useful for very different results. If you want to get across town on the subway system, the road map is not very helpful. If you want to find a particular street while walking, the subway map is almost useless. In the same way, NLP suggests, each human being develops "maps" of reality which help them to get the results they are used to getting. None of these maps are exactly the same as the real world, and none of these maps is exactly the same as another person's map; they are just guides to help us get the results we want.

We filter what we see, hear and touch, in order to create our own maps out of these experiences. Psychologists Daniel Simons and Daniel Levin conducted an extraordinary study to demonstrate how our brain fools us into seeing what we expect to see. Imagine you are walking down the street and a stranger stops to ask you for directions. While you're talking to him, two men pass between you carrying a large wooden door. After they move on, you finish giving the directions, and the stranger advises you that you've just been the subject of a psychology experiment. He asks you if you noticed anything odd after the men with the door passed between you. He then explains that he is not really the person who asked you for directions! The original person who asked for directions actually walked off behind the door, and was replaced by your current interviewer. The original man now re-appears; he is a different height and build, has different clothes on, and has a different voice. But amazingly, when this is done as an actual experiment, over half of the people approached in this way do not notice the substitution occurring (Simons and Levin, 1998). What they "see" is not just what is in front of their eyes. It is even more a result of what they expect to see. The experiment demonstrates that much of what we "see" is fabricated by our mind in order to fit with what we *think* must be happening.

A resilient person understands that their way of thinking about the world was just one choice, and there may be better ways. In disagreements with other people, it is our maps that disagree. It's not that one map is more real; they just have different purposes, and are even based on noticing different things. We do not need to get caught up in trying to prove to our friends that our map is right. In fact, the most useful first step in comparing our maps is to find out where the subway stations are (the places where our maps connect).

2. Each Map Is Designed To Help The Person Reach Their Own (Positive) Destinations

Each person's map is built up to help them meet their own needs and future goals, just as the subway map and the road map each were designed to meet specific needs and help people get to their destinations. Everything that you (and others) have done is the result of some goal or need (to avoid pain, to find more happiness etc). These higher goals or needs are what really "motivate" you. If you can find someone's real goal, you can help them get that in ways that may work even better than what they have been trying so far.

People make the best choices they can, given the map of the world they have at that time (what they believe is possible etc.). They are doing the best they know how to do, within their current maps. You have always done the best you could at that moment. Now, you can develop new and better maps and skills, so that next time you will make even better choices. Since the real world changes, it is an important part of resilience to be able to update your maps in an ongoing way. Ideas that were useful when you were a child may not help you now.

3. Resistance is a Signal to Create Better Rapport

Rapport is the feeling of shared understanding or shared maps that good friends develop. The secret to better relationships is not proving that I am right; it is creating the feeling of rapport. As we will see, better relationships, in turn, are a key to resilience. When someone doesn't co-operate with you, when they "resist" your suggestions, it lets you know that you have suggested something that doesn't "fit" with their map of the world. If you take more time to understand their map of the world (to build rapport) they will be more likely to co-operate with you.

The most important thing to know about what you say is what it means to the person who hears it. You may know what you meant, but other people use their own "map" to understand or "decode" what you meant. If they didn't get the message you intended, it makes sense to say it again in whatever way will best get your real message across to *them*. The way they react to you helps you to know what *they* thought you meant. When others don't respond to you in the way you expected or wanted, it lets you know that their map doesn't match yours in that place.

4. Everything In Life Is Connected

In NLP we understand that life is an interconnected system. All living beings relate to each other and so one person cannot be understood separate from the others around them. One action cannot be understood separate from the other parts of a person's life.

To put this another way, relating to someone is like being on a trampoline together. What you do affects what the other person does, just as what they do affects you. If you want to change what someone else does, first think about how the things *you* have been doing might have caused or allowed them to do what they did. When you change yourself, the system will change.

Of course, in order to change you need a degree of flexibility. Flexibility succeeds better than staying the same, especially since the world itself keeps changing. If what you have been doing so far doesn't work, NLP would suggest it's time to try something different.

An Example of Using The Core Beliefs

In Milton Erickson's work as a psychiatrist, he constantly embodied these basic ideas, but he also lived with them in his personal life. In one case (Erickson and Gilligan, 2005, p 106), another doctor had been seeing Milton as a psychiatry patient. He mentioned to Milton that he was worried about his aunt, a 52 year old wealthy woman who lived alone in Milwaukee. She had been increasingly depressed, even suicidal, but was reluctant to get help, and the weekly visits to her church were her only social support. Erickson mentioned that he would be in Milwaukee at a conference, and the man asked if Milton would be able to visit his aunt.

Erickson called on her and explained that he was a friend of her nephew. Upon being invited into the house, he asked her if he could look around. He immediately realised that every room except one had the curtains drawn and the house consequently had a rather "gloomy" feeling. In that one room – the sunroom – the woman grew a few African violets. Erickson then made a very simple suggestion to her. He noted that her church was important to her and that she always read the notices of births, deaths and marriages in the church newsletter. He commented to her that in these busy times, people rarely get much outside acknowledgement of these important events. He then suggested that it would be very nice if she was able to make some cuttings from her African violets and gift one to each family that experienced one of these life transitions. Then he left.

The woman took up the suggestion and indeed she quickly got very positive feedback from her community. She became, as Erickson expected "too busy to be depressed". On her death some 20 years later, the Milwaukee newspaper carried the headline "African Violet Queen of Milwaukee Dies", and thousands of grateful parishioners attended her funeral.

In this woman's original "map of the world", there was very little point to her life. She had a religious "faith" that was very significant to her in theory, but she had no way of connecting her daily activities to that, except to attend weekly services and read her newsletter. Milton did not argue with her sense of hopelessness, and he did not try to get her to "see a psychiatrist" (something not meaningful to her at all). He merely "utilised" the one daily activity she already enjoyed (growing African violets) and the one social connection she already had (attending church). Using these to create a connection with her, he suggested a way to meet her higher positive intentions, and correctly guessed that the benefits of doing this would affect the whole "system" of her life, including her mood.

Now, we can analyse his strategic thinking, but much deeper than this, much deeper than his use of the four presuppositions discussed above, is his belief in her as a person. She was not in fact his "patient", and he did not treat her as a "project". He genuinely believed that happiness comes from having a sense of the deeper purpose of one's life. He believed that partially because he knew it was true in his own life. In explaining how he helped this woman, Erickson asks us to direct our attention away from "What was the technique used to convince her to change" and to focus instead on "What inner resources did this woman have that Erickson was able to activate." Focusing on what techniques to use is contrary to Erickson's method. Your focus as a person who helps people be more resilient, including a person helping yourself become more resilient, needs to be on what resources this unique individual has that can be utilised. It does not take superpowers: an African violet and a church newsletter can be all the tools needed.

It is also important to notice that Erickson never sees a person as an isolated individual, even when, as in this case, that appears to be their problem. He is aware that human beings do not prosper separate from other human beings, and the demand that they do is an unrealistic expectation of modern society: the meaning of our life inevitably is found in relationship to others.

Key Concept: The Core Beliefs

Resilient people tend to adopt some basic beliefs about life, such as that:
- The map we have of the world is not the same as the territory
- Each person's map of the world is designed to meet some need or positive intention
- Resistance to your proposals is a signal to create better "rapport" or connection with their maps
- Everything in life is connected in systems, and nothing, including problems and including people, exists as a totally separate entity.

Practical Exercises: Day 1

You could treat this book as another interesting set of ideas. My invitation to you is to invest a small amount more over the next 2 weeks and make it work! I know that if you really commit yourself to this time over the next three weeks, it will pay you back in time alone over the very next year! But you will get so much more than free time by committing yourself to this eleven day program. You'll get skills that you can use for the rest of your life! Each chapter will take you perhaps twenty to thirty minutes to fully read. I'm asking you to add another twenty minutes to that time, and complete the exercises that will make that chapter work for you.

In this first day's exercises, you'll get concrete experiences of what a difference adding these core beliefs to your map of the world can make.

A. Pointing Exercise: Stand up with your feet slightly apart. Holding the book in your right hand, bring your left arm straight up in front so it's parallel with the floor. It's important to keep your feet in the same place throughout the exercise. Keeping your feet still, turn your body to the left, pointing with the finger as far as you can turn, until it gets tight. Notice, by the point your hand aims at on the wall, how far round you are pointing. Now turn back to the front. Close your eyes and make an imaginary picture of yourself turning again, but this time going much further. What would you be looking at if you went 30 centimetres further? Sense what it would feel like to be that much more supple and turn that far easily. Also, what would you say to yourself if you could do that easily. Would you be surprised? Once you've really fully imagined that, open your eyes, and, using that same arm, physically turn again to the left, and see how far you go now. Almost certainly, you went much further. The actual territory outside had not changed, but your map of it had changed. Imagining going further created a map of the world in which more was possible.

B. Clarifying maps in a difficult situation. This exercise will be best done with a pen and paper. Think of a situation between you and someone else; a situation where you *didn't* have the sense of being in rapport, or where you were dissatisfied with how things happened. We are not planning to solve this situation right now, but it is probably an example of the kind of situation which you will learn how to solve later on in this book. For now, answer these questions about that situation:
• What were the most important things happening, in your map of the events that happened?
• What were the most important things happening in the other person's map of the events?
• What things did you actually see or hear that the other person didn't even seem to see or hear the same as you?
• In what way did your way of behaving possibly add to the things they did and said which you were not happy with (like the way that your bouncing on a trampoline adds to the behaviour of the other person on the trampoline with you)?
• What positive, useful result were you trying to get to?

- What positive, useful result was the other person trying to get to, in their map of the world?
- Where are three main "subway stations" (places where their map and your map match)?
- What inner resources helped you survive in this situation, and how could you have used those even more fully?

Chapter 2:
How The Brain Reacts To Events

The Brain "Alters" Even Our Most Powerful Memories

On September 11, 2001terrorists flew planes into the twin towers of the World Trade Centre in New York. Watching this event on television would become a defining experience of a generation of Americans. It was a crisis. NLP Practitioners across the USA suddenly found they had thousands more clients. This is the kind of event that people often believe they can remember vividly, exactly as it happened. But not so ….

Neuroscientists, who study how the brain processes events, were immediately doing research on the response to the event. "Within about a week, memory scientists from New York to Michigan to California (now known as the 9/11 Memory Consortium) were querying people on what they remembered. The resulting set of data contained responses from more than 3,000 people in seven cities. Following up with those same people one year and three years later, the researchers found a rapid decline in memory accuracy. After the first year, people's memories of the event were consistent with their initial description only 63 percent of the time." (Pappas, 2011).

The Memory Consortium found that people's confidence that they were remembering accurately was increased by the level of emotion occurring as they remembered, and not by the level of information storage (that is to say, the stronger the emotion, the more convinced the person was that their memory was accurate, but the actual strength of the factual memories did not increase their confidence). Secondly, the memory of this very significant event changed over time in certain standard ways. It was "tidied up" by people's brains. People were asked what they had seen on television that morning. Most people, a year later, could remember watching in shock as first one plane and then another flew into the buildings and then the buildings collapsed. Except … they never saw that on television that morning. By the time people got out their cameras to film the event, the first building had already been hit and was burning, and that is what was available for TV. It was three days before a video taken by a person who happened to be filming at the time of the first incident was found. "In the case of 9/11, people will sometimes claim to have seen live video of the first plane hitting the North Tower of the World Trade Center, Talarico said, despite the fact that such video was not broadcast until days after the attack." Their memory has (completely unconsciously) spliced in images actually seen days later and re-sequenced them to make sense.

So what is really happening with memory?

How Our Experiences Are Converted Into Memories In The Brain

To understand how to respond resiliently even when the world seems to be going crazy, we need to understand how resilience normally works in the brain. What we have been able to learn about brain functioning in the last decade is little short of amazing. We are finally beginning to understand how our brain stores memories as physical changes in nerve cells. One of the most important things that resilient people understand is that the brain itself is already a resilient system. It has great flexibility, and is not stuck in its original way of remembering any event. Learning a little about how the brain adapts helps us to allow that natural process to occur better when we meet a crisis.

In everyday speech we use the word "memory" as if people make a perfect video recording of events in their life, and these recordings are "memories". Scientifically, though, memory means any change in a system as a result of an experience. If you bend a piece of metal and then straighten it again, the metal is not the same - it carries the "memory" of the event.

In a more complex way, our nervous system records changes as a result of the events we experience. For us as humans, memory is our delight and our terror, the source of our happiest reminiscences and our worst nightmares. To live without it (as in Alzheimers disease) is frequently viewed as a fate worse than death. But memory was never designed to do what most of us try to use it for. And once we understand its original design, we can far more effectively use it to remember what we want to remember, and to forget what we want to forget. However one thing we can be certain we can never do with it is the thing that most humans try to do with it every day: to identify which things "really happened" at some time in the past. A memory is a set of changes that happen as a result of an experience, but it is not an accurate record of the experience.

In an animal such as a human being, the brain and nervous system, made up of billions of nerve cells ("neurons"), glial cells and other specialised cells, coordinate actions across the body. To do this, these cells need to react to the world differently as a result of your previous experiences. If a dog bites a child, their brain needs to react differently next time they see that dog. This "plasticity" (changeability) of nerve cells and their synapses (connection points) is what we usually call memory. Memories, then, are changes in the nervous system's functioning which enable you to more effectively respond to current events. These changes in functioning are only incidentally related to the structure of the real previous events which they were initiated in response to. Sure the changes happened as a result of some past experiences, but the changes are not a faithful video recording of those experiences.

So what actually changes when a memory is created? Well, firstly, there are simple changes at the synapses (the gaps between nerve cells, where messages are transferred from one cell to another), and that happens everywhere that nerve cells registering an event are activated. There are increases in neurotransmitter release (neurotransmitters are the messenger chemicals that pass across the gap between nerve cells to carry the messages), and these changes may last for seconds or minutes. Secondly, long-lasting memory depends on wider scale changes such as the physical growth of new nerve cell connections (dendrites), and increases in the number of synaptic connections on those cells.

The most important early changes after a new experience happen in the amygdala and hippocampus, two brain areas in what is called the limbic system, in the centre of the brain. To be exact, the amygdala records the emotional valence (how important it is either positively or negatively - so the amygdala responds especially to things that generate fear, anger, sexual desire, hunger etc.), and the hippocampus records the spatio-temporal coordinates (where and when it happened).

Traumatic Responses explained in the Brain

Not all human experiences are as important as each other. When any new event occurs in your life, a "neural network" is set up in the brain with memories of the event, instructions about possible responses, and an "emotional significance rating" or "valence". If the emotional significance rating is zero, the event is "boring". If the emotional significance is highly positive (an experience of delicious food, a romantic evening, or something absolutely, fascinatingly new, for example) the memory needs to be stronger so you can recreate it or recognise it quickly in future. If the emotional significance is highly negative (something that physically hurt, or was scary, for example) the memory needs to be stronger so you can avoid it recurring in future.

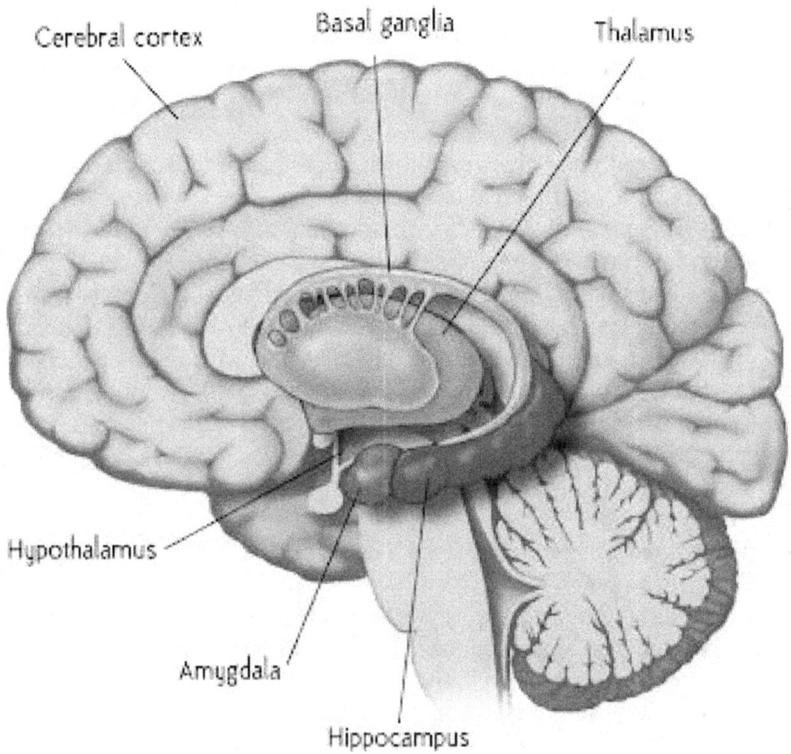

If the negative rating is high enough then at least for some time a panic-style response will occur each time the person thinks about the experience, and the person may have severe difficulty performing normal daily functions. The aim of this "alarm" response is to ensure that if the emergency recurs, the "panic" reaction will override conscious thinking and cause the person to act quickly to save their life. You can understand that in a physical disaster, this is a very sensible body response. While this panic response mostly saves lives, occasionally it results in panic being triggered accidentally by sensory stimuli that are themselves not dangerous (like reading the morning newspaper). Even in that case most people will gradually edit the neural network over the next couple of months so that it no longer interferes with everyday functioning, a pattern called Recovery. Some people have a pre-existing thinking style which makes recovery difficult (e.g. a pattern of constantly checking in case something bad is about to happen again) and they will then continue to have problems long term, a pattern called Chronicity.

Which of the 3 patterns will occur is determined by the pre-existing thinking style and model of the world, previous experience of similar trauma, the severity of the current traumatic events, and the social support available at the time of the current trauma.

The amygdala not only gives emotional significance to a memory, it also signals the brain about the required strength of the memory structure (telling the brain to store more important memories more vividly) and it determines whether an emotional response is strong enough to overide the brain's frontal (conscious) decision-making. With a damaged amygdala, a person tends to engage in more unsafe behaviour and to be unable to assess the seriousness of danger, hunger etc. Damage to the amygdala due to drugs such as alcohol leads to faulty decision-making by heavy users of those drugs, and, by contrast, the stress of PTSD (Post traumatic stress disorder) and other over-activations of the panic system lead to physical hypertrophy (overdevelopment) of the amygdala.

Reconsolidation of Memories from Temporary to Long Term Storage

Remember that the hippocampus stores the data about where and when an event happened. The hippocampus is so central to the initial storage of each new memory that if the hippocampus is damaged, new memories are unable to be laid down, even though memories in the distant past may well be intact (Squire and Paller, 2000). Initially, as a person stores a new memory, the hippocampus is the site at which most of the brain changes occur. Over the first 7 or so days after the event, the memory is primarily stored in changes in the hippocampus, but over the next few weeks it is "reconsolidated", and "storage" of these changes is transferred more widely to other brain areas such as the sensory cortex (the outside of the brain) and even to the cerebellum (the lower brain, which eventually stores behavioural sequences such as walking and dancing, so that these remain intact even if the original sites of these memories in the sensory cortex are damaged by Alzheimers or another condition). Sleep and times of stillness (like meditation or relaxation) seem to be crucial to this process as it is only when the Hippocampus is not getting new memory inputs that it can effectively reconsolidate memories.

The changes in the memory do not stop once it is transferred to permanent storage however. Each time you "think about" a memory, what you do is activate the same neural network as when you first experienced it, or the network of neurons to which that memory has been transferred in the process of reconsolidating it. That means that you "reconsolidate" it again - i.e. by activating the memory, you bring it back into a state of activation, and so over the following 15 minutes or so, the memory has new changes added to it (after all, the principle that "neurons which fire together wire together" still operates, so if you remember an event, your current experiences and thoughts are now connected to the memory of the original event). As we will see, reconsolidation can significantly and permanently alter a "memory" changing the entire emotional valence of the memory (making a memory that was fear inducing become desire-inducing, for example). There is no "undo" function in the brain by which you can go back and reverse previous edits to get to the "original" memory. Memory, then is an active and synthetic process, and memories are changed irreversibly at every re-membering of them.

Reconsolidation of memories eventually organises them into very different places in the brain. At one time in my life, I needed to use my conscious mind to tie my shoelaces. Now days, my "unconscious mind" performs that function. What do I mean when I say that last sentence? I mean that another area of the brain now runs my shoelace tying strategy automatically when it is triggered by the sight of my shoes untied. Even a person severely affected by the memory loss of Alzheimer's disease may continue for some time to be able to tie their shoelaces, because such strategies are stored in areas of the brain less affected by that condition (Schacter, 1996, p 134-137). Such memories are called "procedural memories".

The Mice Who Conquered Fear With Love and Curiosity

In 2014, Dr. Susumu Tonegawa and his team at RIKEN-MIT Center for Neural Circuit Genetics conducted an extraordinary experiment which revealed how the "emotional valence" (whether it feels good or bad) on a memory can be changed in a few minutes of "reconsolidation". (Redondo et alia 2014)

"Both the hippocampus and the amygdala are considered critical for memory formation. We wanted to know whether the memory engram [network] was free to associate with positive or negative valences or whether it was fixed with respect to emotion," said Roger Redondo, who along with Joshua Kim is co-first author of this study, in a press release. "We also wanted to know at what point in the circuit the valence is assigned to the engram, in the hippocampus or the amygdala."

Their experiment takes a few sentences to explain, but it is worth it! The first part is a kind of preparation. The experiments were conducted on male mice, who were placed in a room they had never seen before, and divided into two groups. One group received a mild electric shock on their foot while the other group was allowed to socialize with a female mouse. So the two groups of mice both formed memories of the room, but some formed memories of fear and some formed memories of pleasure. Using a biomarker (a chemical called released into the mice brains to mark out the areas of the brain where new connections were growing), the scientists genetically labelled neurons that were active during the formation of either memory. The team then used "optogenetics" to activate the same set of neurons. This involves shining a light from an LED or laser source outside, through the mouse head - if you hold your hand up in front of a strong light you can see that it shines through the tissue, so this is not surprising. When this light strikes the chemically marked out area in the mouse brain, it triggers the neurons in that area to fire, basically activating the memory network from outside. When the neurons were activated, the mice showed the same response as they did when they originally experienced the event. The mice that had been shocked avoided the room where it had happened, and the mice that had met female mice moved towards the room. the researchers could see the activated circuits inside the mice brains and actually identify the memory of the event, in the hippocampus, and (in mice where this was marked) its connection to the emotional response in the amygdala (to different parts of the amygdala depending on whether the experience was positive or negative).

Next, the researchers gave the mice a new experience, in a new place. The (male) mice who got the mild shock the first time were introduced to some female mice. As they were showing interest in these female mice, the researchers activated the old memory "engram" in the "dorsal dentate gyrus" of the hippocampus. This old memory of being shocked in the room was now connected to the new experience of being interested in the opportunity of meeting the female mice. To the observers' fascination, they could see the memory network changing. The old connections into the fear area of the amygdala were eliminated, physically dissolved, and new connections were made into the curiosity/desire area of the amygdala. Finally the mice were placed back in the room where they had originally been shocked, but this time they immediately showed interest and looked around with positive curiosity. Their memory of the room had changed. Observing the process, the scientists could see that the old memory (or the negative "valence" of the old memory) was simply deleted. The record of being in the room was now associated with positive feelings, essentially creating a new memory.

The effective sequence is to have the mice create a powerful enough positive emotional state, and then, while they are feeling that positive state, to reactivate the place memory of the original event which had been fear-associated. the researchers commented that to transfer this technique to humans, we would only need a way of reactivating the place memory in the hippocampus. In traditional Cognitive Behavioural Therapy this "extinction" of the unpleasant response is done using prolonged "gradual exposure" techniques. In NLP we do this with the much faster process known as "anchoring" (a precise application of classical conditioning as done by Ivan Pavlov with dogs). That will be explained in normal English in the next chapter.

Reconsolidation Requires Sleep!

For now, the part I want to draw your attention to is the reconsolidation of temporary memories into the cortex (outer brain) permanent storage areas. This happens during sleep, and has two steps. In the first step, which happens in deep sleep, the temporary memory is activated and transferred to the new cells. In the second step, which happens in REM sleep (rapid eye movement or dreaming sleep) the new memory is cross-referenced with all other relevant memories, so it can be used. "Generally, earlier dreams in the night include memory fragments from recent experiences, whereas later dreams incorporate memory fragments from increasingly farther back in the past…. dreaming exposes a mechanism whereby emotional issues can be worked through and behavioral strategies can be developed and adjusted with reference to experiences from the preceding days as well as older experiences." (Paller and Voss, 2004, p.667).

People who watched the 911 attacks in New York on their television in 2001 first stored those memories in the hippocampus, with a strong amygdala response. It was scary. Over the next weeks as they slept, they reorganised that memory and reconsolidated it into their long term storage. As they did this, their brain connected the memories from the first morning with the images of the first plane flying into a building, seen three days later on the same television. Recognising the logical sequence, their brain edited the memory so that the video of the first plane was stored immediately before the video of the second plane in sequencing. Over the next year, they thought about the events of that morning again and again, and each time the memory was re-edited, until a year later only 63% of the facts they "recalled" (e.g. where they were standing when they first heard the news, what they said, who was there at the time) were the same as they were in that first week. For those who were resilient, the re-organised memory served them well, and if anything was probably less emotionally charged than it had been at first. But for those who had chronic (long term) problems, the event became more and more distressing, as they imagined, for example, what it was like to be trapped in these falling buildings; until many of them could now be diagnosed with "PTSD" (Post Traumatic Stress Disorder). In the next chapters we will be learning HOW to intentionally choose which response your brain makes to crisis.

Key Concept: Reconsolidation of Memories

Memories are changes in the brain as a result of experiences. The time, place and sensory events of an experience are stored first in the hippocampus and the emotional significance of the event is stored in the amygdala. Over the next month the memory is reconsolidated into more permanent storage in the wider brain, and this reconsolidation happens during sleep most of all. Each time the memory is re-activated, it is reassessed and reconsolidated.

Practical Exercise: Day 2

Mindfulness Meditation.

1. Allow 20 minutes for this exercise (perhaps set your watch alarm for 20 minutes time). Sit with your back straight and your legs uncrossed (or crossed in such a way as to balance the left/right sensations, for example cross-legged or in a yoga posture). Close your eyes and pay attention to your internal state, including all the images, internal or external sounds and sensations you are aware of. This is not a time to try and change these experiences, but simply to observe, as one might listen to excellent music, watch a beautiful sunset or experience a warm bath. There is no need to choose one thought above another, to search for a particular state, or to theorise about or organise one's mind. This is simply a process of being with whatever state of mind occurs, being aware of it, observing it with fascination. There is no particular aim, and no one sensation, state, or thought is more important than any other. This is an experiment to discover what actually occurs over the 20 minutes.

2. After 20 minutes, open your eyes, return to external reality, reflect on what happened. What states of mind did you enter? Were you able to simply be aware, or did you find yourself thinking about and trying to change what occurred, i.e. making yourself an observer separate from the state you were observing? If you were able to be aware, did you find that your state of mind changed naturally (for example calmed down) without using any technique?

Chapter 3:
3 Responses to Crisis

What Happens In A Crisis

A crisis is a break in the stability of a system. In a person it may be a health problem; in a community it may be an economic recession, in a machine it may be a part that wears down to the extent that the machine doesn't work any more. Things are going along "normally", and then something happens that negatively affects the person, the community or the physical system. Of course, there are no people who never have health problems, no economies that never have recessions, no machines that never wear down. In that sense, crisis is normal. It just doesn't always feel good to us as human beings.

If anyone needs to understand crisis it is those people who are called "first responders" – fire services, civil defence people, armed forces and medical emergency staff who go to the scene of a physical disaster before anyone else. I have worked training first responders for a number of major crisis events around the world, including the wars in Bosnia and Chechnya, the Tsunamis in north Japan and Samoa, and the Christchurch earthquake.

Research on human response to other major crises has important lessons about how some people survive better. Almost half the United States population has at some time faced what psychologists describe as a traumatic event so severe it is outside the normal range of human experience, but only one in twenty develop chronic PTSD problems (Bonanno, 2004, p. 54). Psychologists list the three main types of response to disaster as:

1) Resilience. People feel bad for a while, but they still manage to get good sleep, to eat healthily, and to plan successfully. They quickly get back to high level functioning in the new situation. This is the response we want to encourage most, and luckily in almost all research on natural and human-caused disasters, it is the most common.

2) Recovery. For a couple of months, people may be so distressed that they cannot function in their job, and cannot relax. Then, they bounce back, as their system reassesses the challenge they have been through. This is the second most common response. Even most soldiers who experience severe traumatic events in war will bounce back once they return to a safer environment.

3) Chronicity. People are so distressed that they cannot relax, cannot function in their job, and do not bounce back. The important thing to understand about chronicity is that it results from a failure of the

> normal "bounce-back" mechanisms, and mostly people with chronic problems do not only not recover … they get gradually worse.

How many people fit in each category? Well, lets take the example of the 911 event. A population-based survey conducted one month after the September 11th terrorist attacks in New York City estimated that 7.5% of Manhattan residents would meet criteria for PTSD and that another 17.4% would meet the criteria for subsyndromal PTSD (high symptom levels that do not meet full diagnostic criteria; Galea, Ahern, et al., 2002). However, most respondents evidenced a rapid decline in symptoms over time: PTSD prevalence related to 9/11 dropped to only 1.7% at four months and 0.6% at six months, whereas subsyndromal PTSD dropped to 4.0% and 4.7%, respectively, at these times (Galea et al., 2003 quoted in Bonanno, 2004, p 24). That means that while the "Recovery" pattern was seen in perhaps 30% of people, "Chronicity" levels were around 2%. "Resilience", of course, was the result for 70%.

In disaster situations, these different responses do not depend only on the severity of the problem, but on the survivor's personal coping style and past experiences. In the research by Schnurr et alia (2004), a past history of being a survivor of violence almost doubles the risk of PTSD (177%). Good relationships buffer us from harm, bad ones signal a need for extra support.

Furthermore, the percentage of people who respond to a traumatic event by being disabled with chronic PTSD varies from culture to culture. Also note that in the same research, Japanese ancestry Americans had only 14% of the incidence of PTSD that European ancestry Americans had. Polynesian (in the research, specifically Hawaiian; in many ways the same culture as New Zealand Maori or Samoan) ancestry also reduced PTSD rates to 35% that of other Americans. This means that not all the causes of resilience are individual. Cultural background has an effect, both by shaping peoples individual reaction, and by creating different levels of useful social support.

Resilience is pretty much the core successful human response to disaster that coaching and solution-focused counselling seeks to create. Research also shows that personal resilience is not a set personality trait so much as a set of actions you can choose to take.

Studying Excellence: How Poland Avoided the Recession of 2008

Since 2007, the world economy has experienced the longest recession since the 1930s. But not everyone has been suffering. "Poland is the only country that was not negatively impacted by the recession. We have been calculating that from 2008 until late 2012, we have had almost 16 percent growth," Under-Secretary of State Beata Stelmach says in Warsaw. Rafal Szajewski, team leader for the services section at Poland's Foreign Investment Department, lists three key factors that he believes helped the nation defy a world-wide trend to recession:

a) Careful investment of EU funds instead of getting swept into get-rich-quick banking schemes.
b) Continued purchasing and business activity by a confident middle class.
c) Creating products and services at increasingly high quality and yet maintaining Poland's low prices.

These three factors in turn depend on three "soft skills" – careful goalsetting choices, creating a confident emotional state, and quality improvement by what NLP calls "Reframing". How did Poland get and maintain those skills, and how can you learn to do that in your business too?

Part of the answer is that these soft skills are directly transmitted in Polish business by the profession of coaching. Business coaching does for business what sports coaching does for a sports team. It involves people meeting regularly with someone who guides them to maximise their success. No sports team in their right mind would try to do without a coach. Hiring a coach means focusing on building the resources a business already has. Poland has the highest per capita number of Business Coaches of any country outside North America. The 2012 ICF Global Coaching survey, for example, studied coaches in 117 countries and identified some remarkable differences with Poland. Polish coaches help with personal growth and with maintaining the work-life balance substantially more than coaches in other countries. Polish coaches know that personal skills matter at least as much as specific business planning skills. Polish coaching has strong university backing. I have been teaching coaches in Poland each year since 2007 and have participated first hand in this explosion of coaching. NLP (Neuro Linguistic programming) based coaching training can show you how to build the soft skills of resilience for yourself and then how to coach others to use those same skills.

Patterns of Chronicity

So what individual factors make some 2% of the population have chronic and even deepening problems after these crisis events? The thinking styles that obstruct change and recovery after a traumatic event are of course ones that were learned earlier in a person's life, and with the best of intentions. They are thinking patterns that may even have worked well in the small challenges of the person's childhood, but they do not handle the big challenges of a crisis. The simplest way to deal with them is to show the person how they are operating and have them practice an alternative. It's not very glamorous compared to ten years of psychotherapy, but it's a lot cheaper. Andy Austin lists several of these "patterns of chronicity" and here we have adapted descriptions of seven of his categories.

1. **"What If…" Questions.** Even when things start to feel safe again after the crisis, the person running chronicity patterns asks themselves "Yes, but, what if something really bad happens again?" The positive intention of negative "What if?" questions is to attempt to anticipate and find solutions to future challenges, but by running it on impossible-to-manage scenarios (For example by asking "What if I die horribly?"), the person is locked in panic. Resilient people don't spend all day asking "What if I die horribly?" They focus on planning what they CAN do something about. "Given the situation I'm actually in right now, what is my best immediate goal?"

2. **"Why…?" Question. The second internal question that the person asks is** "Why did this happen to me?" The positive intention of past-related "Why?" questions is to find new meanings, but the person rejects each possible future-oriented meaning and keeps searching as if trying to find a meaning which can change the traumatic event or recreate the past. Resilient people search for future oriented meanings, essentially asking "What can I learn for the future from this?"

3. **Focusing on Problems.** Asking these unhelpful questions focuses the person with chronicity on what was bad in the past and what might be bad in future. One of the ways that resilient people bounce back from crisis is to focus their attention on even small positive events. When they feel even slightly more comfortable, they notice and acknowledge it. By contrast, even though 99% improvement might be made, if the person with chronicity is able to locate just 1% of the problem existing, this will generally be seen as representative of 100% of the problem existing. This means that if you make them a cup of tea and ask them if that feels better, they will tell you that although they like a cup of tea, right now their stomach feels uncomfortable so that they know their feeling is still just as bad. If you ask them to imagine a future time when they feel better, they will explain that they could do that, but they are still able to think about the bad events and feel bad, so what is the point? The positive intention of "Can I still experience the problem?" responses is to detect and respond to danger effectively, but by failing to notice improvement the person continuously reinstalls the entire problem. Resilient people do not keep checking if they can still get the bad feeling. They pay attention to "What feels better?"

4. **The "Maybe" Response.** Because they are habitually focusing on negative parts of their experience, people with chronicity are reluctant

to acknowledge any positive results at all. They fear that they may be just fooling themselves and may soon discover that the tragedy is still just as bad, so when you ask them if something makes them feel better, they often say they are not sure, or preface their answer with "Maybe". The positive intention of "Maybe" responses is to avoid mistakes such as false hope, but by refusing to commit to any specific data, the person can never measure change and can never experience success. "Maybe" seems such a gentle comment, but it is a lock that traps them eternally. The resilient person is able to acknowledge how they feel right now; and is thus able to identify what makes them feel better and do more of that.

5. **Negative Labels.** As the person with chronicity pays attention to their problem continuously, it begins to seem eternally present – to be a thing in itself. Anxiety is not a thing: it is the action of worrying. Trauma is not a thing.: it is the process of remembering an unpleasant event in a specific way. The person with chronicity talks about their traumatic responses as if the responses are "things" rather than actions. "I have Trauma", "I have PTSD", "I have a Wounded Inner Child", "I have a Clinical Depression." The positive intention of Negative labels is to explain what is happening by labelling it, but the result is that the processes being discussed seem permanent, damaged and even become personified as malevolent, and so are unable to be simply changed. The resilient person is more likely to say "I have been feeling …" or "I have been experiencing …" rather than "I have a …." Or "I am a …."

6. **Being "At Effect" rather than "Being At Cause".** By being "at effect", I mean that the person with chronicity experiences emotional problems as external things that are happening <u>to</u> them, rather than being something that happens by way of the things they do. They feel like other things cause what is happening in their internal experience, rather than that they participate in creating their internal emotions and thoughts. A person "at effect" will seek treatment rather than seek change. They will look for explanations for their problems such as genetics, that suggest the challenges are unsolvable. Questions such as "Will this process work for me?" or statements such as "Your process didn't work for me." And "The process worked for a day and then the problem came back." also presuppose that the problem and the outside process are 100% responsible for how they feel, and the person themselves is 0% responsible for their own results. It's as if a person wanted to learn a new language and I showed them a process for studying. They ask "Can you promise me that the process will work for me?" I would say, of course, "I believe it will, but only if you actually use it". The positive intention of "At Effect" responses is to explain what is happening without being at fault, without feeling blamed for their problems, but by not allowing for the possibility of their responses affecting their internal experience, the person makes it impossible to change their experience. Because

resilient people are focused on what they CAN change, they feel as if they are far more in charge of their positive results. Resilient people thus have what Positive Psychology researcher Martin Seligman (1997) called "an optimistic explanatory style".

7. **Nocebo Responses to Help.** As a result of this cognitive style, the person with chronicity has a "nocebo" (I will not please; the opposite of placebo) response to helping processes. Any therapeutic process designed to get them to change actually triggers a cascade of unconscious "Why?" and "What-if?" questions followed by focusing on the problem and thinking of it as an eternal and uncontrollable external element of their life. Consequently, they have an "uncontrollable" negative response to all interventions designed to actually help them change, although they permit interventions which maintain their problem. A small percentage of all medical clients in clinical research trials will complain that they get headaches etc. due to an inert "pill". This nocebo response also occurs with psychological interventions. It looks like what Freud called an "Abreaction". This may lead to quite severe panic reactions: e.g. vomiting, convulsing, running out of the room screaming, uncontrollable crying. The positive intention of "Abreaction" responses may be to protect the person from feared results of the change process, but it blocks all change. Like any reflex response, abreaction cannot be controlled in the immediate situation but can be changed by earlier interventions into the thinking style that generates it, as we will learn.

One way to understand chronicity is that it is a response of "learned helplessness". Steven Maier and Mark Laudenslager exposed two groups of rats to electric shocks (not a very nice experiment, but we can still learn from the consistent results). One group of rats could control the shock with a lever; the other group had no way to control it. In a short time, the immune system of the rats with no control was in collapse while the others stayed healthy (Ornstein and Sobel, 1989, p 151). In another study, Maier and Martin Seligman found that dogs who had been put through this experience (of being unable to control the shocks) developed a style of behaviour they called "Learned Helplessness". In subsequent experiments, the dogs would not even jump out of an area which gave them shocks; they had given up on being able to prevent the problem. Seligman followed up these experiments by studying human beings. He found that humans with this "learned helplessness" approach respond to stressful events (such as failing a university exam) by becoming depressed (Seligman, 1997).

So what do resilient people do instead of these patterns of chronicity? The American Psychological Association says research suggests that research supports several "Ways to Build Resilience", in order to cope with traumatic events. You'll notice that these are essentially the mirror image of chronicity. How to actually put these recommendations into practice is the subject of the next chapters:

10 Ways to Build Resilience
The American Psychological Association
(https://www.apa.org/helpcenter/road-resilience 2019)

Make connections. Good relationships with close family members, friends or others are important. Accepting help and support from those who care about you and will listen to you strengthens resilience. Some people find that being active in civic groups, faith-based organizations, or other local groups provides social support and can help with reclaiming hope. Assisting others in their time of need also can benefit the helper.

Avoid seeing crises as insurmountable problems. You can't change the fact that highly stressful events happen, but you can change how you interpret and respond to these events. Try looking beyond the present to how future circumstances may be a little better. Note any subtle ways in which you might already feel somewhat better as you deal with difficult situations.

Accept that change is a part of living. Certain goals may no longer be attainable as a result of adverse situations. Accepting circumstances that cannot be changed can help you focus on circumstances that you can alter.

Move toward your goals. Develop some realistic goals. Do something regularly — even if it seems like a small accomplishment — that enables you to move toward your goals. Instead of focusing on tasks that seem unachievable, ask yourself, "What's one thing I know I can accomplish today that helps me move in the direction I want to go?"

Take decisive actions. Act on adverse situations as much as you can. Take decisive actions, rather than detaching completely from problems and stresses and wishing they would just go away.

Look for opportunities for self-discovery. People often learn something about themselves and may find that they have grown in some respect as a result of their struggle with loss. Many people who have experienced tragedies and hardship have reported better relationships, greater sense of strength even while feeling vulnerable, increased sense of self-worth, a more developed spirituality and heightened appreciation for life.

Nurture a positive view of yourself. Developing confidence in your ability to solve problems and trusting your instincts helps build resilience.

Keep things in perspective. Even when facing very painful events, try to consider the stressful situation in a broader context and keep a long-term perspective. Avoid blowing the event out of proportion.
Maintain a hopeful outlook. An optimistic outlook enables you to expect that good things will happen in your life. Try visualizing what you want, rather than worrying about what you fear.
Take care of yourself. Pay attention to your own needs and feelings. Engage in activities that you enjoy and find relaxing. Exercise regularly. Taking care of yourself helps to keep your mind and body primed to deal with situations that require resilience.
Additional ways of strengthening resilience may be helpful. For example, some people write about their deepest thoughts and feelings related to trauma or other stressful events in their life. Meditation and spiritual practices help some people build connections and restore hope. The key is to identify ways that are likely to work well for you as part of your own personal strategy for fostering resilience.

Key Questions: Installing an Antidote to Chronicity Patterns

Just pointing out the difference between chronicity patterns and resilience patterns does make a difference, but if you already recognise chronicity-style thinking in your own daily life, you are probably now wondering where the magic fix is. The search for a special magic that will make the patterns go away right now … is part of the problem though. Like any new behaviour, developing more resilient patterns of responding to challenges takes time and attention. As you notice from the description of chronicity above, it means learning to ask yourself better questions.

Ibrahim Senay, Dolores Albarracín and Kenji Noguchi at the University of Illinois (Senay, Albarracin and Noguchi, 2010, p 499-504) gave research subjects challenging tasks, and had them say one of two very different type of comment to themselves before starting. One type of comment was "I will do this" (an affirmation). The other was "Will I do this?" (a question). In several different experiments, the results were the same. Those who asked the question were more motivated, more focused and more successful. Furthermore, they reported different subsequent thinking about their goals. In one study, for example, subjects had a goal of going to the gym regularly. Those instructed to say "I will" reported later that they felt motivated (for example) "Because I would feel guilty or ashamed of myself if I did not," whereas those instructed to say "Will I?" reported that they felt motivated (for example) "Because I want to take more responsibility for my own health." Paradoxically, the affirmations had a kickback effect of making the people think about what they did not want to happen, whereas the questions focused them on what they wanted to happen. The researchers noted that questions open the person to possibilities while affirmations close the mind to other choices. Questioning invites you to explore; affirmation tells you what is and ignores the ability to find unexpected or more useful results.

We can see this questioning style of internal dialogue in Milton Erickson's work. Milton Erickson continuously quotes his own internal dialogue before any new success as "I was wondering…" He does not use self-affirmations, he uses self-questioning. For example in his collected works, in a discussion with Ernest Rossi, he mentions how he developed the ability to write whole articles during his sleep, unconsciously. He says "I wondered if I could write editorials. If I did not recognize my words on the printed page, that would tell me there was a lot more in my head than I realized. Then I had my proof that I was brighter than I knew." (Erickson, 1980, p 114) Later, he describes how he gave himself a transcendent personal experience: "I was in the backyard a year ago in the summertime. I was, wondering what far-out experiences I'd like to have. As I puzzled over that, I noticed that I was sitting out in the middle of nowhere. I was an object in space….It was the most far-out thing I could do!" (Erickson, 1980, p 129).

One NLP process that installs a useful questioning style as a meta-strategy in a challenging situation is the Core Questions Process described by Steve Andreas in his new book "Help With Negative Self Talk" (Andreas, 2010, p 82). The basic idea of this process is that we are continuously sorting our experience / deciding how to respond by asking ourselves unconscious questions. Sometimes these questions are structured so that they deliver only unhelpful answers (like, for example "Why does this always happen to me?"). You can identify such unhelpful questions and install more useful questions that are better designed to meet your intention. My own version of this installation process follows.

The Key Questions process (following) is useful for helping a person consciously create a new more effective guiding question for a specific context in their life, where they want to change their responses.

Key Concept: Responses to Crisis

Crises are a normal part of life where equilibrium is interrupted. The responses to crisis can be classified as: 1) Resilience (approximately 70%), where the person is in discomfort but able to continue with daily life. 2) Recovery (approximately 28%), where for a time they are unable to manage but they bounce back. Chronicity (approximately 2%) where the person's state steadily gets worse. Resilience is characterised by making relationship connections, taking action towards positive and realistic goals, and getting a bigger perspective that helps focus on positive events. Chronicity is characterised by asking unhelpful internal questions ("What if …?" and "Why?") and by focusing on negative events and labelling the problem.

Practical Exercise: Day 3

Key Questions (A simple process for deciding what you'll ask of life!)

1. Choose The Context. The habitual questions we ask ourselves, almost unthinkingly, as we are in a situation, guide our decisionmaking in that situation. Some questions do not focus us on what can be changed, but instead actually prevent us being able to change. What situation, or what context do you want to find a new key question for. (e.g. "at work", "my relationship with my kids", "dealing with a colleague"). As you think of that situation, imagine stepping back into your body there. Notice what you see through your eyes there, what you hear, and what you feel in your body. Be aware of how you are deciding what actions to take.

3. Elicit The Old Question. If there were a question that quietly guided all your behaviour in this context, what would it be? Now think of that question. Check that when you say that question to yourself, it reminds you of the situation. (You're checking it feels like thinking of that situation itself. Often your conscious memory will give you a polite watered down version of the real question e.g. "Why is this not working?" rather than the real one e.g. "Why do I always screw this up?".

4. Find The Positive Intention. If you knew, what is your unconscious mind's positive intention in asking this question in this situation? If you think of a negative intention (like "to get me worried") ask yourself "And when it gets me that fully and completely, what even more important thing do I get through that?"

5. Create A New Key Question. What question that would be even more effective in getting you the positive benefits you want in that situation? Often the simplest question will be some version of "How can I more fully get that positive intention? ". "Why" questions tend to be backward looking and ineffective, and questions that have a yes/no answer (where yes is positive and no is negative, e.g. "Will this person like me?") often create anxiety.

6. Install The New Question. Having a chosen a better question, I'd like you to step back into your body in that situation, and say the new question to yourself -actually say it aloud now, as you imagine being in that situation. Notice that when you're in that situation now, the new question is quietly at the back of your mind, guiding your behaviour, and check that that feels much more enjoyable! Imagine a future time, when you'll be in that situation again, and check how asking that new question changes the way it feels.

Chapter 4:
Creating A Resilient State Of Mind Quickly

The Song On The Radio

To get different results in a crisis, we saw, you need to ask yourself better questions and focus on more useful events. That's all very nice, but most people know that in the real world they are not always in the state of mind where they feel like using what they have learned. Your state of mind determines what you can do to change you results. In this chapter you'll learn important secrets about how to change your own emotional state almost instantly.

Sounds too good to be true? Consider this everyday experience then. Everyone has had the experience of listening to a song on the radio, a song that you haven't heard for years and years… and then suddenly getting back the whole feeling of what it was like all those years ago, suddenly remembering the sound of friends voices, the images of the places where you first heard the music and so on. Just as an anchor holds a ship steady in place, so the music is an "anchor" that re-members (joins together again) all the sensory components of that earlier experience. The music becomes a natural way to recreate the state of mind you were in when you first heard it.

Imagine what it would be like to be able to choose the state of mind you are in for each task you want to do, by "playing your own music". "Anchoring" can give you that ability.

The White Rabbit

In the 1920s, two American psychologists demonstrated the power of anchoring with very young children. John Watson and Rosalie Rayner worked with an 11 months old baby named Albert, in an experiment that would now be considered very unethical. Albert was a happy little boy who rarely cried. However, like most young children, he was afraid of loud noises, and when a steel bar was struck with a hammer near him, he would shake, fall over and cry. First, Watson and Raynor gave Albert a pet furry white rat to play with. Albert was delighted. The second time they gave him the rat, however, they struck the steel bar with the hammer as he reached for the rat. Albert burst into tears. After dong this a few times, just seeing the rat caused Albert to shake and burst into tears. In fact, after that, Albert was frightened of white rabbits, and even large balls of cotton wool.

Four years later, John Watson redeemed himself by putting his new understanding to good use. He and Mary Cover worked this time with a three year old boy named Peter. Peter had a fear of rabbits and similar animals (one developed "naturally" rather than installed by psychologists). This time, Watson gave Peter his favourite food – milk and crackers – and showed him a rabbit (at a distance) while he was happily eating and drinking. Gradually, while Peter enjoyed the positive anchor of the food, Watson brought the rabbit nearer until Peter was quite happily playing with the pet rabbit. As the experiments were concluded, Peter announced to Mary Cover "I like the rabbit". (M. Cover Jones, 1924)

Anchoring Happens All the Time.

Anchoring can happen in any sensory system. A specific sound (auditory), sight (visual), taste (gustatory), smell (olfactory), or touch (kinesthetic) can anchor the entire state of mind originally associated with it. Some time ago, I was having an argument with a close friend. We'd been arguing for about an hour and it felt pretty hopeless. We were sitting next to each other, each of us hurt and doubtful about the other's intention. Absent-mindedly, I put my arm around her shoulder as if to give her a hug. Suddenly her whole body vibrated and then became more relaxed. "What happened?" I asked.

"I don't know," she said, "but I just remembered that you care about me." I nodded. Her saying that also reminded me! Within ten minutes we had sorted out our conflict. The touch of my arm around her shoulder had been in exactly the same place, with exactly the same pressure as at times when she knew I cared about her. It recreated the whole state. When she told me what happened, I was anchored back into a similar state. And, in case you ever had any doubt, feeling caring or loving is the very best state to be in to sort out any conflict.

Actually, anchoring is happening all the time. Even words are just anchors. The word "cat" means something to you because it reminds you of times you've seen/touched/smelled a cat. Your parents deliberately anchored it for you, by saying the word "cat" exactly when you were next to one. After a few times, just their saying that word brought back the whole memory of a cat.

Reading this book anchors you into a certain state. That's how people come to enjoy reading. If, when you were young, you sat on someone's knee and they lovingly read you a book, then in time you'll get those good feelings just looking at this book. Good anchoring is the key to feeling the way you'd like to feel about any situation.

Some people wonder "how long" an anchor will last. One answer is this: how long will the anchor of the word "cat" last? If you don't use it for ten years will it still work? The answer is that anchors will last forever unless you decide to change them. That song that reminds you of that happy time in the past can always be available, if you like, to take you back to fully enjoy the richness of your life experiences.

Mary Kay Ash, manager of the multimillion dollar company Mary Kay Cosmetics, used anchoring with her staff. When she met a new staff member, she would greet them with a smile and say "Hi, how are you!" She explained "When a new employee answers, "Uh, pretty good. How are you Mary Kay?" I'll say, "You're not just good, you're great!" This generally gets a faint smile, and the next time I see him or her and ask "How are you?" he or she will say, "I'm great." Each time afterward, the response is, "I'm great!" and the smile gets bigger and bigger. If you act enthusiastic, you become enthusiastic." (Williams and Williams, 2003, p 341-342) This process of anchoring every new employee was so important to Ash that she once declined an invitation from President Ronald Regan because she had to be in Dallas greeting the new employees there, and setting up what we would call in NLP the anchor of "I'm great."

In a controlled research study published in Germany (Reckert, 1994), Horst Reckert describes how in one session he was able to remove students' test anxiety using this simple technique, described below. In another study, John Craldell discusses the use of anchoring to access a "self-caring-state" useful for adult children of alcoholics (Craldell, 1989), and in a third study, Mary Thalgott discusses the use of anchors to support children with learning disabilities (Thalgott, 1986).

Of the hundreds of examples of anchoring principles applied in an innovative way, without the name "Anchoring", one stands out for me. It is Ellen Langer's study of two groups of elderly men (aged 75-80 years), at Harvard University. For 5 days, these two comparable groups of men lived in a closely supervised retreat centre out in the country. One group was engaged in a series of tasks encouraging them to think about the past (to write an autobiography, to discuss the past etc.). The other group was engaged in a series of tasks which actually anchored them back into a past time (1959). They wrote an autobiography only up to 1959, describing that time as "now", watched 1959 movies, had 1959 music playing on the "radios", and lived with only the artefacts available in 1951. Before and after the 5 days, both groups were studied on a number of criteria associated with aging. While the first group stayed constant or actually deteriorated on these criteria, the second group dramatically improved on physical health measures such as joint flexibility, vision, and muscle breadth, as well as on IQ tests. They were anchored back to being 50 years old, by the sights and sounds of 1959 (Langer 1989).

Using Anchors In Your Daily life

Now that you understand the concept of anchoring, you probably realise that you can "tidy up" the anchors in your life so that you are anchored into the state of mind you want to be in, and so that your children are also anchored into useful states of mind. For example:

1.   Check that the places you relax and sleep are set aside for relaxation. Do not do high energy activities such as watching intense television programs, in bed. Do not argue and try to resolve conflicts in bed, or try to balance the accounts in bed. Remove unpaid accounts etc. from sight in the places you want to relax. Keep beds for relaxation.
2.   Have anchors for high energy in the morning to wake yourself up, and anchors for relaxation in the evening to calm you down. Doing the same sequence of events before bed each day, at roughly the same time, helps relaxation. Slow down your voice and movements in the evening to help relax; speed up n the morning to help energise.
3.   Find out what music gets you into states of inspiration, calm, love, confidence and creativity. Notice what pictures (for example photos of places where you have enjoyed being) create these states for you. Choose to make these anchors available where you want those states of mind, at home or at your work.
4.   Create positive anchors with touch by holding and hugging your friends, partner or family members when they are in strong positive states, rather than just when they are sad. If this touch becomes associated with positive states of mind first, then it can be used to recreate these positive states when they are needed. Make touch a positive anchor so that you can recreate those good feelings as needed.

Creating An Anchor For Confidence

Because anchoring is always happening, and is not a conscious process, most people have picked up a few anchors they could do without. In my work as an NLP Practitioner and teacher, I've assisted many people to change such experiences anchoring. Here's one example.

Jenny asked if I could assist her to be in a better state during written school examinations. She said she got incredibly anxious about exams: they were associated with a lot of bad memories - times she'd "failed" at school. It puzzled her, because she knew that there were some times when she knew the subject she was studying fully, but completely forgot it in the exam situation. She knew she was smart enough to learn the subjects she wanted to learn, but something about the tests "triggered her off." For Jenny, exams - even just seeing a room set out for an exam - anchored her into a state where she felt hopeless. All her resources, her confidence and intelligence, weren't available once she saw the test.

The first thing I did was to get into rapport with Jenny. The first step in helping someone else set an anchor for relaxation is for their unconscious mind to allow them to relax and that requires them to feel safe and understood. In other words, rapport is what enables you to help someone else create anchors successfully. To invite someone to change their state of mind, remember, the first step is always to join them in the state they are in now. I told Jenny I could understand how difficult it was and how frustrating it must be to realise that she knew the answers but was not relaxing enough to remember them.

Next, I explained to Jenny that I'd use anchoring by having her make a gesture with her hand, to resolve this challenge. I would have her remember a time when she felt truly confident and relaxed, step back into that experience and create an "anchor" for it. Once she'd set up this anchor, just using that hand gesture would re-create that confident state. In that way the feeling of confidence and relaxation would be automatically and unconsciously associated with the examination she was sitting. Jenny was sceptical but ready to try anything. I asked her to choose a gesture she could make with the hand that was free when she wrote an exam (her left hand). That gesture needed to be unique –something she would not usually do. She chose pressing her thumb and second finger together.

Next, I asked Jenny to remember a time she had felt really relaxed, maybe on holiday. I had her step into her body at that time and feel what it felt like, see what she saw, listen to the sounds there, and listen to anything she might say to herself in that situation. I watched her carefully as she re-experienced this time. As she got back into the state of relaxation fully (rather than just "thinking" about it) there were changes in her:

- Voice quality (her voice became "softer")
- Eyes (her pupils dilated)
- General posture (her body relaxed and extended)
- Expiration - inspiration (her breathing slowed down)
- Skin (her face flushed more and was softer)

I needed to see and hear these changes to know that Jenny was fully in the state she wanted. As she re-experienced this state of relaxation, I had her make the gesture with her hand. I asked her to stand up and stretch, to "clear the screen" of her mind. Next I went through the same procedure with a time Jenny had felt incredibly confident (a time from when she was skiing). Again I watched for the non-verbal shifts that told me she was in a confident state before having her make the same hand gesture. I had now connected this gesture to two resourceful states.

After clearing the screen again, I had Jenny make the gesture, and feel that state of both relaxation and confidence combined. I told her "Now, try and think of that exam you have coming up."

Jenny frowned. "It's funny" she said, "I'm finding it hard to even remember what worried me. But it feels totally different."

"Try and get back the feeling you used to have," I suggested. I like to make sure the person's brain has made the connection.

"No, I can't do it," she said after a pause.

"You used to be good at that", I reminded her.

"That's right, but now it just feels relaxed."

"For the First Time In My Life ...."

I asked Jenny to think ahead to her exam, and asked what happened when she made the gesture and thought of that. "Well," she smiled, "I can imagine it being okay: but I don't know. I'll tell you on Monday." I asked her to remember that when she used the anchor, it was important first of all to let go of any unhelpful anchors that she was already using. For example, it would be a good idea for her to stretch her body and take a deep breath, and then use the resource anchor. She asked me how long the anchor would "last". I explained "You know how sometimes you hear a song on the radio and it brings back the whole feeling of what it was like years ago when that song first came out?" She nodded. "Well, let me ask you, how long will that anchor last?"

She laughed. "The rest of my life." She said nodding in understanding.

She saw me the next day with some dramatic news. "Last night," she bubbled over, "I went to study for the exam. And I thought, "This'll be a drag, because I've always found exams hard. But I used that anchor, and somehow it was completely easy. In fact I enjoyed it so much I studied everything for that test and went on to study for the next one as well."

I nodded. "So I guess now you're convinced that Friday's test will go okay."

"Well, I'll wait and see."

The Monday after the test she was finally willing to accept it. "For the first time in my life, I felt totally relaxed in an exam." she told me.

To me as the person who assisted Jenny, what's most exciting is that she overcame her "" with her own inner abilities. Her brain already knew how to be relaxed and confident. It just needed to make the connection from this state of mind to the exam situation.

Using Anchoring For Yourself

You can use this process yourself immediately. Let's say you would like to feel relaxed while communicating with people. Luckily, you probably have a time each day when you are already relaxed. Choose a time when you are very relaxed (perhaps just before you fall asleep), and try the following: at that time each day, press your left thumb and forefinger together and say to yourself in a calm voice: 'relaxed and confident. (There's nothing magic about pressing your thumb and forefinger together, it just happens to be something you're only likely to do in this state, so it probably doesn't have any contradictory states already anchored to it.) After only two or three days, you'll be able to approach someone, press your thumb and forefinger together in just the same way, say 'relaxed and confident' to yourself in the same calm voice... and you will relax. The more you use this technique, the more powerful it will get.

Key Concept: Anchoring

Our state of mind is largely a result of the responses we have to what we see, hear, taste, smell and touch physically, because each of these experiences can connect us to remembered responses and feelings. By choosing to use any of these sensory systems, you can create an anchor for a positive experience which will assist you yourself or your child to shift into the state of mind you are wanting at a particular time.

Practical Exercises: Day 4

A) Anchoring Checklist: Run through the following checklist to make sure you are using anchoring to create the states of mind you want to.

1. Are the places you relax and sleep set aside for relaxation and free of high stress activities?
2. Do you have a standard sequence of events before bed each day, at roughly the same time; a time when you slow down movements and voice to relax?
3. What music gets you into states of a) inspiration, b) calm, c) love, d) confidence and e) creativity? Do you have it available when you need it at home and at work?
4. What pictures (for example photos of places where you have enjoyed being) create states of a) inspiration, b) calm, c) love, d) confidence and e) creativity for you? Do you have these available when you need them at home and at work?
5. Do you create positive anchors with touch by holding and hugging when others are in strong positive states.

B) Setting An Anchor: Choose a time in the next day, when you are in a powerful positive state, laughing or having fun doing something you enjoy. Use a unique and specific hand gesture, with a specific pressure, that you can remember later. Repeat the touch exactly at a second time, soon after, when you are still feeling good. Later, perhaps on another day, use that touch before focusing on some task that would usually be mildly challenging, and notice the change.

Chapter 5:
Finding Better Meanings

Things Don't Always Go Exactly The Way You Want

Like it or not, things do not always go smoothly in your life. Everyone faces ups and downs in their life, but some people have an attitude that enables them to bounce back quicker, to treat each challenge as an opportunity instead of a block. In the last two decades, for the first time psychologists have actually researched what makes some people happier than others. How do happy people respond differently to the challenges of daily life? How can you become one of these happy people?

The answer is not about what happens to us. Happy people have just as many challenges in their life as unhappy people. The answer is in the map of what happens that each of us makes up: the explanations we give to ourselves to make sense of what happens. When my son Francis was three years old, he was running across the other side of a large room one day, when he tripped and fell flat on his face. Indignantly, he looked over to me and said, "Why didn't you catch me!" This misunderstanding of the situation is amusing in a three year old. It is dangerous in a thirty year old. In Francis three year old map of the world, I was supposed to make him happy. This way of explaining things leaves him feeling as if he depends on external events to turn out well, in order for him to feel safe and happy.

Having someone catch you when you trip is what psychotherapist Gregory Bateson would call first order Resilience. Second order Resilience involves changing how you experience it even if you fall flat on your face.

Raising An Optimistic and Happy Child

Psychologist Martin Seligman calls second order Resilience "learned optimism". He explains (1995, p 44-45) "In the struggle to cure syphilis in the first decade of the century, Paul Ehrlich concocted a drug, 606, that worked by poisoning *Treponema pallidum*, the spirochete that causes syphilis. It was called 606 because before it Ehrlich concocted 605 other drugs, none of which worked…. Children need to fail. They need to feel sad, anxious, and angry. When we impulsively protect our children from failure, we deprive them of learning the 606 skills…. And if we deprive them of mastery, we weaken self esteem just as certainly as if we had belittled, humiliated, and physically thwarted them at every turn."

In a study of learned optimism, Seligman tested 500 members of the first year class at the University of Pennsylvania. He found that their scores on a test of optimism were a better predictor of their actual grades during the next year than either intelligence test scores or high school grades. This suggests that teaching your child how to reframe experiences helps their success at school better than extra homework or study time!

Resilience does not deny the pain or the actual challenges of life. It "reframes" the situation – like putting a different frame around a picture. In this new "frame", even pain, while recognised, has far less significance. In a very real sense, Paul Ehrlich never failed at all while searching for a cure for syphilis; he continued to utilise feedback until he reached his outcome. "Not having found a cure" is the actual sensory event he experienced, but "failing" or "having checked another chemical off the list" are just different "frames" or meanings.

Dr Milton Erickson, one of the expert therapists studied by the developers of NLP, gives a very clear example of this "reframing" (Rossi ed. 1989, p176-179) . One day his 3 year old son Robert fell down the back stairs, split his lip and impacted a tooth into his jaw. The boy screamed in pain and terror, staring horrified at the blood all over the pavement. Milton Erickson's first comment to was "That hurts awful, Robert! That hurts terrible." Robert nodded, crying in terror. "And it will keep right on hurting. And you really wish it would stop hurting." Robert nodded again, feeling his suffering was completely understood. "And we don't know if it will stop in one minute, or in two minutes." Robert agreed. This also was very true. Erickson continued, pointing to the blood which had so terrified Robert "That's an awful lot of blood on the pavement."

So far, all Erickson had done was to acknowledge what was really happening, speaking Robert's deepest fears and thoughts. Milton had also checked that Robert wanted his help. To do all this, he used the skill we will call reflective listening in a later chapter, and he now had Robert's full attention. Milton continued "Is it good strong red blood?" It was a harmless enough question. Robert wasn't sure. Milton explained that if it was good strong red blood, it would turn the water pink when they washed his face clean. They went into the bathroom, and washed up Robert's face, and sure enough, the water turned pink. Robert was very impressed. Milton began to carry on talking about the stitches Robert would get, just as his older brother Allan and older sister Betty Alice had had. Milton speculated as to whether Robert would be able to get as many stitches as they had had. Robert was very curious about that. He was now totally engaged in creating the outcome of healing.

Reframes of Happiness

Seligman's research showed that people who are sustainably happy interpret life's positive results and life's challenges in a particular way. They assume that positive results are permanent (this good result will continue), pervasive (this good result will affect many other events) and personal (this good result is evidence that I am good). They assume that negative results are temporary (this challenge will pass), specific (this challenge only affects a small area of my life) and situational (this challenge is a result of something in the particular situation). He called these assumptions an optimistic explanatory style.

People who get depressed in crises, who suffer chronicity, make the opposite assumptions –for example, that bad things are always happening to them because there's some fatal flaw in their nature, and those bad events will ruin everything. (Seligman, 1995, p 163).

Adults, Seligman is saying, can teach an optimistic explanatory style to their children by restating challenges as temporary, specific and situational. In the example of Erickson and his son Robert, above, Erickson acknowledged Robert's pessimistic perception of his own crisis (which Robert feared was permanent and had damaged him profoundly) and then communicated that:
- Robert's pain was temporary (one or two minutes in fact)
- Robert's pain was specific and situational (because Robert had good strong red blood, itself a permanent pervasive positive resource).

Erickson emphasised (Rossi ed., 1989, p179) "At no time was he given a false statement, nor was he forcibly reassured in a manner contradictory to his understandings." Reframing is not telling your child that they "should" think happy thoughts – that would increase the feeling of powerlessness. It is acknowledging their unhappiness and then **offering** them another way to think about what the situation means.

One famous New Zealander described a traumatic event on his first day at secondary school: an experience which, sixty years later he said "still affects my whole attitude to life". He said "When I first went to Grammar, we all had to go along to the gymnasium to be assessed for sporting potential. This gymnastic instructor, who I regard as one of the more unpleasant teachers I ever had anything to do with, looked at me when I stripped off. I clearly remember him staring at me with scorn and saying, "What will they send me next?" He told me I had a bulging rib cage and my back wasn't straight, everything that was terrible about my physical appearance and set-up. I was mortified and this created in me an enormous sense of inferiority."

At first, this experience shattered the young boy's confidence, but at home he reframed the experience. He explained, "I think this incident built up in me - I was after all only 11 at the time - a determination that I would become competent in something." His family were very involved in a movement that we would recognise today as being related to NLP. The movement was New Zealand teacher Herbert Sutcliffe's "School of Radiant Living". They studied nutrition, herbalism, energy healing and the use of "affirmations". Sutcliffe's motto was "Faith in goodness will produce good things. Faith in abundance will draw conditions of abundance around you. Faith in health will establish health in body and environment."

On the 29th of May, 1953, that boy, now grown to adulthood, stood at 8848 metres above sea level in the snow covered Himalayas, atop the highest mountain in the world. Edmund Hillary had become the first person to climb Mt Everest. A childhood challenge, reframed into a vision of success, had led Edmund Hillary to achieve an outcome that others thought impossible. (Booth, 1993, p33)

Don't Think Of Your Left Foot

Edmund Hillary's belief in himself became a powerful "suggestion" to his unconscious mind. Each thing you say to yourself becomes a suggestion as powerful as any a hypnotist could make. NLP trainer Tony Robbins emphasises that: 'the quality of your communication with yourself is the quality of your life!" (Robbins, 1988). He points out that your unconscious mind is listening to and reacting to every internal comment, even the ones you didn't intend it to hear. For example, if you say to yourself: 'I'm aware of my left foot' several times, you'll find yourself very aware of your left foot. However it's also true that if you say to yourself: 'I'm not aware of my left foot', you'll also become very aware of it.

The unconscious mind can only understand the statement: "don't think of your left foot', by thinking of the left foot! Why is this useful to know? Well, it means that if you tell yourself: 'I'm not going to get anxious. I'm not going to worry about this...' over and over, guess what? You'll find your unconscious mind is more and more aware of the worry. Instead, it's more effective to tell yourself: 'I'm relaxing more and more. I'm getting more and more comfortable. I'm more and more aware of the places in my body that are at ease.' And then you will relax more.

Meaning Reframe

Reframing is based on the awareness that events in themselves don't have one specific meaning. Human beings give them meanings. The NLP term for such "meanings" is "frames".

The question behind reframing is "What else could this situation mean, that would be *useful*?" It's a question that all highly successful communicators ask themselves. Oprah Winfrey is one of the world's most successful television presenters. Yet when she was a child she was the victim of horrific sexual abuse by her cousin, her uncle and her mother's boyfriend. Lots of people told her that *meant* that her life was damaged. For years she believed that she was to blame. Oprah eventually decided it could have another meaning: it *could mean* that she was able to speak out and help people around the world who have lived in fear. Her talk-back TV show achieves exactly that. When she began running it, people told her she couldn't succeed, especially when Phil Donahue was already so successful in the business with *The Phil Donahue Show*. "They said I was black, female and overweight. They said Chicago is a racist city and the talk-show formula was on its way out." For Oprah, that just meant that she didn't need to try and be the top show. She explained "I felt completely uninhibited to speak with my own voice." (Williams and Williams, 2003, p 92-99). In 1986, Oprah Winfrey made a syndication deal with King World productions and debuted on national TV. She made $30,000,000 the first year.

That's the power of meaning reframing. To restate, events in themselves don't have one specific meaning. Human beings give them meanings. When someone tells you that their husband died last week; you don't know what that "means". You only know what the sensory specific event was. The meaning depends on how they filter that event. They may feel happy that they are free of an oppressive relationship, or glad that their husband is free of pain, or grief stricken that he is gone, or guilty that they didn't do more for him. Meaning is a result of our filtering processes, and a meaning reframe offers new filters.

In offering a meaning reframe, it will often help to reflective listen (to pace the person's own frame) first; to say "So you thought that the event meant…. I think it could mean…." When the person feels that you have understood their meaning, they are more willing to listen to yours. Oprah Winfrey might say "So you thought my unhappy childhood meant I would be damaged for life. I think it means I'm in an ideal situation to speak out on behalf of other children and get some changes."

When the second biggest car rental firm promotes itself with the slogan "We're number two; we try harder!", that's a meaning reframe! And when Pepsi-cola takes on the century old "classic" Coca-cola empire with the slogan "Pepsi, the choice of a *new* generation", that too is a reframe. Such moves seem chance acts of creativity, until you understand their linguistic structure. And after all, ALL business is reframing (or is that another reframe?).

Another example of Milton Erickson's ability to reframe or find new meanings for experiences is given in his work with a young woman named Jane (Erickson and Rossi, 1989, p 47, p 77). Jane came to Erickson saying that she had a childhood without loving parenting, where her father was always absent and her mother felt resentful about being "left with the children". Jane told Milton that she was afraid that now she herself would be unable to be a good mother, because she never experienced good parenting in her own childhood.

Milton responded by building a sense of connection first. He acknowledged her distress. Then he reminded her about a time when, as a child, she stubbed her toe on a door. It hurt terribly, and she never thought at the time that there could be any positive meaning to such a bad experience. But now, as a parent, she will be able to use this memory to make her more understanding of what it is like when her child suffers one of the inevitable bumps of early childhood. Milton says "Maybe someday you will talk to a little girl about her stubbing her toe. You will really want to know what a stubbed toe felt like. Isn't that right?"

Milton explains to a fellow doctor, Ernest Rossi, about this process of reframing, "You don't really alter the original experience, you alter the perception of it, and that becomes the memory of the perception." Jane will now remember this moment of childhood "pain" as a moment of learning about how to be a good mother. And Milton is explaining to her that all those memories of not having a happy childhood can be useful in that same way. She knows what she never got, and she knows how important that is to her own child.

Notice also that he offers the reframe rather than telling Jane she must believe it. He doesn't say to Jane "One day your own daughter is certain to get hurt and your stubbing your own toe will shave been a good thing because you will need to remember what it felt like." He says "**Maybe** some day you will talk to a little girl about her stubbing her toe. You will really want to know what a stubbed toe felt like. **Isn't that right**?"

Steve Gurney's Imagination

Steve Gurney is one of New Zealand's most famous sportspeople – a triathlete. Here's how he describes reframing his experience at a "Coast to Coast" triathlon in 2003 (Gurney, 2003):

"The more racing years that I notch up, the more I am learning that the keys to winning are the psychological aspects. ***"Attitude determines altitude,"*** says it all. None more so than this year. There was a huge weight on my shoulders. Bristling and ready to pounce was a small gang of young successors, determined to take my Coast to Coast crown off me. Hungry young bucks like Neil Gelately, Richard Ussher, Marcel Hagener, not to mention the old adversaries like Eric Billoud. The media was also hungry and fuelled the drama with headlines like "Who will be heir to the Gurney throne" Subaru [the sponsor] simply expected a win, a compliment I know, but what pressure!"

"I'd like to share with you a small but extremely powerful story of how I used mental attitude through Neuro-Linguistic-Programming (NLP), to boost my performance in this year's Coast to Coast. It's a story about turning a negative into to a positive,.... Converting "worry" into a "challenge"! Instead of being scared of the competition I wanted to "relish in the challenge" I was worried about the mountain run. Despite being a handy runner and getting plenty of run training under my belt I'm not as fast over Goat Pass as Gelately. Historically, I would emerge from the mountain run with a deficit of 8 to 10 minutes on the leader. It then requires a mammoth effort for me to close this gap before the finish line.,...very stressful! (Of course I could run through the mountains faster than the leaders, but it is a matter of efficiency. I need to carefully pace myself to race at a speed that I can maintain for the entire 11 hours, not just a 3-hour mountain run. I could win the mountain run, but blow up before the race finish line)"

"I enlisted the help of my NLP guru, Richard Bolstad for some help with this one. To summarize, the solution lay in blowing apart my belief that I always trail the lead runners by 10 minutes. Bolstad powerfully pointed out to me that reality is whatever I imagined it to be, and in fact, with a little work I could alter my beliefs to be more powerful and positive. I visualised the lead runner to be "just around the corner" ahead of me, possibly even behind me, and not the dreaded 10 minutes that I was imagining. It worked a treat! I emerged from the run 1 minute ahead of Gelately!! My best mountain run to date!! The mechanism is one of positivity, fun and enjoyment. This releases endorphins and other natural "go-fast" chemicals that enhance focus, concentration and more efficient use of muscles and blood glycogen."

The breakthrough that Steve describes happened once he realized that the only sensory reality in his experience of exhaustion on the mountain run is that he is running on a stretch of road and cannot see the other runners. The theory he has that this means that he is getting further and further behind the front runner, and that it will be harder and harder to catch up after this section of the race, is just a theory, just a "meaning". I simply pointed out to him that if he was going to imagine something happening that he couldn't actually see, and that imagination was having an effect on his running, then he was allowed to choose what he imagined. His imagination was framing his experience in a way that created negative results. Once he imagined other possibilities, he got entirely different real world results from his body. He didn't deny the reality that he was running on the road by himself. He merely changed the frame of what that might mean. Notice that meanings are not rational. They are not facts, although they actually influence future facts. You can choose what meanings you hold to. That is reframing.

Key Concept: Reframing

How resilient you are depends more on the meaning you attribute to events than it does on the actual events that happen. Resilient people have an optimistic reframing style which:
- Pays attention to what they want instead of what they want to avoid
- In desired situations, thinks of their results as permanent, pervasive and personal
- In undesired situations, thinks of their results as temporary, specific and situational
- Finds positive meanings in all results

Practical Exercise: Day 5

1. Identify a challenge you face in your life at present. Write a description of that challenge in two columns. The first column is where you list the "sensory specific events". That means exactly what you would see or hear on a video, or be able to touch in a sculpture. It does not include whether the event is "good" or "bad", "right" or "wrong", "easy" or "hard", "likely to continue the same way" or "likely to change soon". It does not include any conclusions about what kind of person you are, or anyone else is, about whether other people are thinking certain things inside, or feeling certain emotions. Those are all aspects to list in the second column. The second column is where you list "meanings". Meanings include your theories about why the event happened the way it did, whose "fault" it is, your theory about what will happen in future

as a result of the event, your theory about how important or trivial the event is, how good or bad the situation is, and what hidden patterns this one event may be part of. These are all "meanings" or frames. For this exercise to work you need to be very careful that the first column does not include even any hints about the meaning.

2. Notice that everything in the second column is made up or accepted by your choice. If you made up another meaning, it would be no more "true" but it might well be more useful. Now ask yourself "What else could these sensory events mean". List on paper at least ten other possible meanings. It doesn't matter how crazy they seem. The main point of reframing is to help your mind loosen the apparent connection between the sensory events and the "one true meaning" that you assumed previously. Notice that each of these different meanings will focus your attention on different parts of the experience and give you different choices about what to do next. Choose which meaning would be most useful to experiment with over the next week (you can always go back to your original theory if you don't enjoy the new frame).

Chapter 6:
Setting Goals That Work

The Failure Of Most Goal-setting

Focusing on realistic goals is not just a recommendation for resilience: it is almost a definition. When I teach resilience, I find that most people *believe* that they know how to set and achieve goals. However when we actually check people's real life results, we find that most people, most of the time, do not set and achieve goals at all.

Richard Wiseman (2009, p 88-93) did a very large study of goalsetting. He tracked 5000 people who had some significant goal they wanted to achieve (everything from starting a new relationship to beginning a new career, from stopping smoking to gaining a qualification). He followed people up over the next year, and found firstly that only 10% ever achieved their goal. It wasn't just bad luck. Dramatic and consistent differences in the way they thought made those 10% stand out from the rest.

Those who failed tended either to think about all the bad things that would happen or continue to happen if they did not reach their goal (what NLP calls away from motivation, and what other research calls counterfactual thought) or to fantasise about achieving their goal and how great life would be if they somehow magically got what they wanted. They also tried to achieve their goal by willpower and by attempts to suppress "unhelpful thoughts". Finally, they spent time thinking about role models who had achieved their goal, often putting pictures of the role model on their fridge or other prominent places, to remind them to fantasise and wish they were like those people. Although the unsuccessful 90% were convinced that these strategies would help them, none of these techniques worked, and furthermore, the successful 10% did not waste their time doing these things.

The key to the problem 90% of us have lies in a series of complete misunderstandings about what a goal actually is. I am going to suggest that, mostly, the 90% failed because they did not actually have goals. In this chapter I want to distinguish goals from five completely separate things: values, directions, problems, affirmations and competitive targets. All of these five things may be useful, and using several of them at once is perfectly workable, but these last five are not goals. Starting "goal-setting" with one of the other structures in mind means not actually achieving the results that goal-setting promises.

Problems

The first thing that Wiseman found unsuccessful people did was to think a lot about how bad things have been for them, and how they are not where they want to be. Wiseman says "For example, when asked to list the benefits of getting a new job, successful participants might reflect on finding more fulfilling and well-paid employment, whereas their unsuccessful counterparts might focus on a failure leaving them trapped and unhappy." (Wiseman, 2009, p 92) Focusing on problems and what we don't want is paying attention to the past. It feels very different to focusing on the goal, outcome or solution to those problems, and it has very different, and less useful, results.

In 2000, Dr Denise Beike and Deirdre Slavik at the University of Arkansas conducted an interesting study of what they called "counterfactual" thoughts. These are thoughts about what has gone "wrong", along with what they could have done differently. Dr. Beike enlisted two groups of University of Arkansas students to record their thoughts each day in a diary in order to "look at counterfactual thoughts as they occur in people's day-to-day lives." In the first group, graduate students recorded their counterfactual thoughts, their mood, and their motivation to change their behaviour as a result of their thoughts. After recording two thoughts per day for 14 days, the students reported that negative thoughts depressed their mood but increased their motivation to change their behaviour. They believed that the negative thoughts were painful but would help them in the long term.

To test out this hope, the researchers then enlisted a group of students to keep similar diaries for 21 days, to determine if any actual change in behaviour would result from counterfactual thinking. Three weeks after completing their diaries the undergraduate students were asked to review their diary data and indicate whether their counterfactual thinking actually caused any change in behaviour. "No self-perceived change in behaviour was noted," Dr. Beike told Reuters Health. Counterfactual thoughts about negative events in everyday life cause us to feel that we "should have done better or more," Dr. Beike said. "These thoughts make us feel bad, which motivates us to sit around and to feel sorry for ourselves." So what does work? The study found that "credit-taking thoughts", in which individuals reflect on success and congratulate themselves, serve to reinforce appropriate behaviour and help people "feel more in control of themselves and their circumstances." (Slavik, 2003).

It is quite common, when teaching someone how to be more resilient, for them to explain to me that their goal is "Not to be anxious". This contains no different information that the statement "My problem is being anxious". It does not tell me what they want instead. NLP Trainer Steve Andreas had a great metaphor for this. Imagine, he said, that you get into a taxi and tell the driver "I don't want to be here." And when the driver, in a puzzled way, says "Yes, but where do you wasn't to be instead of here?" you reply "Well, somewhere else." There is no point in the driver moving her or his car until you learn to state a goal.

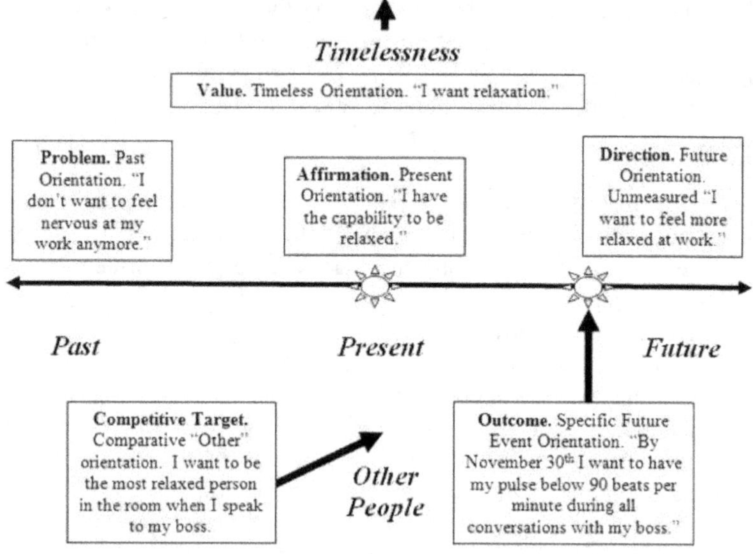

Values

The next most common response when I ask a person about their goal, is for them to tell me a single word for a state of mind that they enjoy and value. "I want happiness." they say. In Wiseman's research, the most successful people were able to list concrete, specific benefits they would get from their goal, rather than just say that they would "feel happy". They had what Wiseman calls "an objective checklist of benefits" and made these "as concrete as possible", often by writing them down. He notes "… although many people said they aimed to enjoy life more, it was the successful people who explained how they intended to spend two evenings each week with friends and visit one new country each year." (Wiseman, 2009, p 91- 93). To explain the difference, if a client tells me that their goal is to be happy, I usually explain that there are pills that can do that for them easily. When they tell me they want to be happy without drugs, I tell them that avoiding all activity may be a really safe choice. Usually by that time they begin to get specific and explain exactly what they will be doing and thinking and how they will feel about that.

"Happiness" is not an end result, a goal. It is a state of being, a valued experience that could be experienced in many different contexts. To be able to check that they have achieved a goal, we need to know what the person's target context is, and what specific evidence they would need to know that they had achieved this desired state of being. A goal is not a value, it is a specific event which expresses or allows the expression of a value. Values are immensely useful to understand. Knowing a person's values enables them to check whether their goal will allow them to embody those values or not. Since values are what motivates a person to action, knowing them enables us to know whether they will actually want to achieve their goals or not (whether they will value those goals). A goalsetting process is like a ladder that a person climbs to reach what they want. A value is a wall that they would like to get to the top of. Leaning the ladder of goalsetting against the wrong wall means that the person is wasting their energy. But just choosing the right wall does not get you far in the process of climbing. Values tell you where it is worth going. Goals tell you how you will know you are taking steps in that direction.

Affirmations

Psychologists Joanne V. Wood and John W. Lee from the University of Waterloo, and W.Q. Elaine Perunovic from the University of New Brunswick (Wood, Perunovic and Lee, 2009), first asked 249 research subjects to fill in a short questionnaire (the Rosenberg self-esteem scale) designed to analyse their self-esteem and to say how often they said positive things about themselves, on a scale from 1(never) to 8 (almost daily). 52% gave a rating of 6 or higher. These 52% of subjects, who already had high self-esteem, reported that they already often said affirming things to themselves. They reported using positive self-statements before exams (85%), before giving a presentation (78%), to cope with negative events (74%), and even sometimes as part of their everyday routine (23%). On average, they felt that such statements were helpful. Those with low self-esteem also claimed that such statements sometimes helped them, but they reported that affirmations more often made them feel worse. To find out why, the researchers did two follow-up studies.

First, they asked their subjects to write down anything they felt or thought in a four-minute period. The recruits included equal numbers of students with high or low self-esteem and half of each group were told to say to themselves, "I am a lovable person", every 15 seconds, on the cue of a bell rung by the researcher. Afterwards, they completed several questionnaires. Two of these were designed to assess their mood, including questions such as "What is the probability that a 30-year-old will be involved in a happy, loving romance?" and "Would you like to go to a party?" Another set of questions rated their current self-esteem by asking them to say which of two adjectives they felt closest to – e.g. valuable or useless, nice or awful, good or bad. As you might expect, the students with higher self-esteem had higher, happier scores on all three questionnaires than those with low self-esteem. After saying the affirmations, there was no statistically significant change in their scores. But for those subjects who already had low self-esteem, the effect of the affirmations was dramatic and negative. They felt worse after saying these words, had more negative beliefs, and had lower expectations of success. Their self-esteem scores were almost halved as a result of trying to use affirmations.

The researchers explain the result by saying that everyone has a range of ideas they are prepared to accept. Messages that lie within this boundary are more persuasive than those that fall outside it - those meet resistance and can even lead to people holding onto their original position more strongly. If a person with low self-esteem says something that's positive about themselves but is well outside the range of what they'll actually believe, their immediate reaction is to dismiss the claim and feel even worse. Statements that contradict a person's current self-image and basic model of the world, no matter how positive in intention, are likely to trigger mismatching thoughts.

Wood concluded that affirmations only work in situations where people make very specific statements that are impossible to argue with, or where none of their major beliefs are challenged. For example, people may be better off saying "I choose good gifts for people" rather than "I'm a generous person". Put in the terms of my communication skills text Transforming Communication (Bolstad, 2002), positive statements are better worded as sensory specific "I messages" rather than as judgments. Wood and colleagues cautioned that "outlandish, unreasonably positive self-statements, such as "I accept myself completely," are often encouraged by self-help books. Our results suggest that such self-statements may harm the very people they are designed for: people low in self-esteem." (Wood, Perunovic and Lee, 2009, p 865)

In the third study, subjects were asked to consider the statement "I am a lovable person" and either to focus only on ways in which it's true, or to consider ways in which it is and isn't true. After the task, people with high self-esteem benefited from focusing only on the positive side of the statement, but those with low self-esteem felt worse about themselves if they dwelled only on positives, and better if they were asked to take a more balanced approach. Wood suggests that if people with low self-esteem are asked to think only positive thoughts, and find it difficult to block out negative ones, that merely certifies their belief that they aren't measuring up to standards.

NLP trainers Robert Dilts and Judith DeLozier (Dilts and DeLozier, 2000, p 24) recommend what they call "affirmations". However, Dilts and DeLozier's examples of affirmations are all current reality based. Put another way, Dilts and DeLozier's examples are all process oriented e.g. "It is possible for me to be healthy and well," "I have the capabilities to be healthy and well," rather than outcome based "I am healthy and well." The above research suggests that since their affirmations don't challenge the client's "reality" they are more likely to be received positively.

In relation to goals, what this research shows is that stating your goals (what you want to happen in the future) as affirmations (what you appreciate about what is happening now) is counterproductive. Affirming your current strengths, resources, achievements and gratitude is very useful, but it cannot replace goalsetting.

Goalsetting Works Better Than Positive Fantasies

Although focusing on the problem you have had does not lead to success, neither does *merely* fantasising about the future success. Lien Pham and Shelley Taylor at the University of California did a study where a group of students were asked to visualise themselves getting high grades in a mid-term exam that was coming up soon. They were taught to form clear visual images and imagine how good it will feel, and to repeat this for several minutes each day. A control group was also followed up, and the study times of each student as well as their grades in the exam were monitored. The group who were visualising should, according to proponents of "The Secret" DVD and the "Law of Attraction", have a clear advantage. Actually, they did much less study, and consequently got much lower marks in the exam (Pham and Taylor, 1999).

This result is very consistent. There are now a large number of research studies showing that "The secret" or "The law of attraction" (visualising your outcome and then letting go and trusting that the universe will provide it) impedes success. Gabrielle Oettingen at the University of Pennsylvania has done a number of studies showing the same result. In one study, women in a weight-reduction program were asked to describe what would happen if they were offered a tempting situation with food. The more positive their fantasies of how well they would cope with these situations, the less work they did on weight reduction. A year later, those women who consistently fantasised positive results lost on average 12 kilos less than those who anticipated negative challenges and thus put in more effort (Oettingen and Wadden, 1991). Oettingen followed up final year students to find out how much they fantasised getting their dream job after leaving university. The students who fantasised more reported two years later that they did less searching for jobs, had fewer offers of jobs, and had significantly smaller salaries than their classmates (Oettingen and Mayer, 2002). In another study she investigated a group of students who had a secret romantic attraction, a crush, on another student. She asked them to imagine what would happen if they were to accidentally find themselves alone with that person. The more vivid and positive the fantasies they made, the less likely they were to take any action and to be any closer to a relationship with the person 5 months later. The result is consistent in career success, in love and attraction, and in dealing with addictions and health challenges (Oettingen, Pak and Schnetter, 2001; Oettingen, 2000; Oettingen and Gollwitzer, 2002).

Directions

The last two types of non-goal are at least moving in a useful direction. However they measure themselves not against a desired future success, but against some aspect of the present situation. As it implies, a direction only tells you the direction, and not how far the person wants to get to by a certain time. A person may say, I want to earn more money next year than this year (meaning that if they earn one cent more, their goal has been achieved) or I want to be more relaxed when talking to my boss (meaning that a pulse rate just 5 beats per minute below their current level of anxiety would be goal success). In some ways this is very valuable information. A positive "towards" motivated direction is a generative plan (i.e. it keeps generating new actions) rather than one that leads only to one specific point. Some people would benefit by having more direction, rather than only specific targets. In that sense, directions are similar to values; they give an ongoing check that you are doing something useful. They are not goals.

Competitive Targets

Imagine that a person tells you that their problem is that they want to remain relaxed while they talk with their boss (problem), and they value calmness (value), and they know they have the ability to relax (affirmation). Then they explain "So my goal is that when I am speaking to my boss, I will be the most relaxed person in the room." Probably, you would immediately identify that even if they can measure their bosses relaxation (and they need to be able to do so to know if they achieved this "goal", in order to check that they are even more relaxed than the boss) this "goal" has some unhelpful consequences.

Firstly, it divides their attention, because usually a person measures their own success. In this case they must measure both their own success and the success of the others in the room, and then effectively compare these. It divides their attention between the two competitors. Secondly, the goal is almost worthless, because technically they will still have achieved it if they find that they are (for example) fractionally less than the psychological mess that their boss is. They are setting a goal and allowing their bosses level of success to decide how much they will reach for. The same two problems occur with all competitive goals – being "the highest earning person in my business", having "a closer relationship than any of my family" etc. Given the obvious ineffectiveness of such competitive goals, why do new clients choose them?

The answer is a social mythology around the value of "Competition." The belief many parents, teachers and team leaders have is that trying to do better than someone else leads to success, and even "builds character." David and Roger Johnson (in Kohn, 1986, P47) reviewed 122 research studies on how co-operation or competition affect success. In only 8 of these studies did competition seem to help. In most of the studies, people co-operating were far more successful, <u>and</u> felt better about their achievement at the end. Airline pilots who are competing against each other fly less safely than those who co-operate. Scientists who are competing for honours make less scientific advances. A study of business people showed that the most successful business people were the least competitive, dramatically contradicting what was being taught in business training. John Simmons and William Mares (in Kohn, 1986, p213) review studies of co-operatively run workplaces showing that they produce more than hierarchical and competitive ones. The reason is very simple. Competition requires paying attention to how the other person is doing. Success requires paying attention to how <u>you</u> are doing. The competitor is like a person running a race while looking over their shoulder to check the others (a problem which actually obstructs even sports success, and feeds what is known as competitive anxiety, where the sportsperson can perform better in practice than in the actual sports "competition". If you want to succeed - personally <u>and</u> in your group - the answer is to focus on your own achievements.

But doesn't business success, and thus economic survival, depend on the competitive, dog eat dog system of capitalism? The truth is surprising. Like everywhere else, competition and win-lose solutions simply obstruct economic success. One person who was very clear about that was W. Edward Demming, the business adviser famous for his central involvement in the economic miracle in post-war Japan. Asked whether competition wasn't the factor that made America great, Demming replies "No; it was co-operation. Competition is our ruination. We've been on the decline for decades; we're on the decline. The decline will continue till we learn." Business consultant Edward de Bono calls competition a "dangerous and seductive trap that limits and restricts business thinking." He gives specific examples. "When Kodak ventured into the instant camera business a few years ago, analysts marked down Polaroid stock. But in fact, Polaroid's sales increased because Kodak now had to advertise instant cameras....The more antique shops, the more the area will be visited by antique buyers...."

Goalsetting – The Secret Of Success?

Goals, then, are stated in the positive, they are sensory specific, they are measurable, they are time-specific and the time they refer to is in the future, and they refer specifically and only to the unique achievements of the person setting the goal.

The complete inventory of successful strategies that Richard Wiseman's research found fits neatly into a "SPECIFY" model for outcome or goal setting (Bolstad, 2002).

Sensory Specific: Firstly, the most successful people did imagine achieving their goal, and were able to list concrete, specific benefits they would get from it, rather than just say that they would "feel happy". They had what Wiseman calls "an objective checklist of benefits" and made these "as concrete as possible", often by writing them down. He notes "… although many people said they aimed to enjoy life more, it was the successful people who explained how they intended to spend two evenings each week with friends and visit one new country each year." (Wiseman, 2009, p 91- 93)

Positive: Secondly, they described their goal positively. Wiseman says "For example, when asked to list the benefits of getting a new job, successful participants might reflect on finding more fulfilling and well-paid employment, whereas their unsuccessful counterparts might focus on a failure leaving them trapped and unhappy." (Wiseman, 2009, p 92)

Ecological: That's about as far as the research results coincide with the "Secret". For example, one surprising result of the research by both Gabrielle Oettingen and Richard Wiseman is that it pays to think about challenges you may face in achieving your goal (even though that may feel unpleasant at the time). After thinking about the positive benefits of achieving their goal, the most successful participants would "spend another few moments reflecting on the type of barriers and problems they are likely to encounter if they attempt to fulfil their ambition…. focusing on what they would do if they encountered the difficulty." (Wiseman, 2009, p 101) Oettingen trained people to do this process, which she calls "doublethink" and NLP would call checking "ecology". She was able to increase their success dramatically just with this step.

Choice Increasing and Celebrated: Related to this NLP concept of ecology is the fact that successful goal-setters made sure that they felt as if their progress was bringing them rewards rather than limiting their choices and creating work. They did this most of all because "As part of their planning, successful participants ensured that each of their sub-goals had a reward attached to it" so that it "gave them something to look forward to and provided a sense of achievement." (Wiseman, 2009, p 93)

Initiated by Self: Successful goal-setters have a plan. They do not leave their goal up to "the law of attraction" or to someone else who will save them. Wiseman notes "Whereas successful and unsuccessful participants might have stated that their aim was to find a new job, it was the successful people who quickly went on to describe how they intended to rewrite their CV in week one, and then apply for one new job every two weeks for the next six months." (Wiseman, 2009, p 91)

First Step Identified: Wiseman found that it was particularly important to break the goal down into small steps and manage one step at a time. "Successful participants broke their overall goal into a series of sub-goals, and thereby created a step-by-step process that helped remove the fear and hesitation often associated with trying to achieve a major life change." (Wiseman, 2009, p 90-91)

Your Resources Identified: In NLP we encourage people to identify both internal and external resources. Wiseman's research studied only external resources, most especially friends, colleagues and family. "Successful participants were far more likely than others to tell their friends, family and colleagues about their goals.… Telling others about your aims helps you achieve them, in part, because friends and family often provide much needed support when the going gets tough." (Wiseman, 2009, p 91). Internal resources are memories of positive experiences that you can anchor (see chapter 3).

Reality-Testing Your Goals In A Crisis

Clearly, one of the reasons that positive fantasies reduce success is that they may not even be achievable at all. In business, people often have another mnemonic for remembering goals – SMART (Specific, Measurable, Achievable, Realistic, Timely). The emphasis here is on setting goals that can be achieved, because in business you do not get paid for wasting your time on impossible dreams. In a crisis, what is achievable may shrink dramatically. More than ever, you need to be SMART!

My mother was in Christchurch, New Zealand, when the earthquake of 2011 hit. As her house violently shook, every cupboard door was thrown open and everything that could be smashed was smashed. The electricity, water supply, sewage system, phone line and gas supplies of the city were suddenly cut off and would not be back on for days. The roads were damaged and mainly impassable. All food that depended on supermarket and home refrigeration systems was rotten within a few hours. Suddenly, career and educational goals, relationship conflict resolution goals, status achievement goals and artistic or scientific goals became irrelevant for most people. Realistic goals were things like getting clean drinking water to last the next few days; digging a sanitary toilet hole in the backyard garden; clearing a safe and sheltered place to sleep for the night; planning exactly what to do when aftershocks happen; checking on the first aid needs of people in the immediate city block and saving any lives that could be saved safely.

People who have practiced goalsetting consciously can adapt the process to think through their priorities in the crisis. Those who have just been acting in a routine will have challenges because the routine is gone. That's why it is important to practise now, even if you are generally pleased with the results you currently get in your life!

Key Concept: Goalsetting

Goalsetting is different to just thinking about your problem, just identifying the values that are important to you, just affirming your ability and fantasising nice results, or even that setting a direction of a person you want to achieve more than. The most successful goalsetting has eight steps:
Sensory specific. Describe in detail when you will achieve it and what you'll see, hear and feel.
Positive. Focus on what you will get, in positive terms, instead of on the problem situation.
Ecological. Check the other consequences of achieving it.
Choice increasing. Check that it expands your choices rather than narrows them.
Initiated by you. Focus on your actions rather than the responses of the system and others.
First step identified. Understand that several steps may be needed. Do one at a time.
Your resources identified. Creatively use external resources, and inspiring internal memories.
Feedback. Use all results as feedback to help you decide what to do next.

Practical Exercise: Day 6

Setting An Outcome

1. Start by allowing yourself to dream. Think of your life over the next five years and imagine all the things you'd like to have happen in it. Put any doubts or "back to reality" comments away for now and simply imagine what could change. Check all areas of your life; career, family, health, personal growth, and so on. Write down a collection of the dreams you come up with. Take at least ten minutes to dream.

2. Choose one of the dreams that particularly attracts you. Now, with a pen and paper, go through the following process, altering your description of the goal, and making notes as appropriate about the implications of the goal.

Sensory Specific: When exactly will you have this achieved by? Write down the date you'll have achieved it. Now imagine yourself on that day. Step into your body and see what you see through your eyes, hear what you hear through your ears, feel what you feel through your body. What specific things in what you see/ hear/feel let you know you've achieved your goal? Write these down.

Positive: Check that you've written your goal in positive language. If it says what you'll *stop* doing/feeling, or what you *won't* have, be, do, then check "If I don't have that, what is it I *will* have instead?" Rewrite your goal if needed.

Ecological: When do you want this outcome in your life especially? Are there any times/situations you don't want it? If so write those down. Know where you *will* have it. Secondly, when you have achieved this goal, what else in your life will change?
- What will you gain if you have this?
- What will you lose or give up if you have this?
- How will this affect your relationships and what others do?

If you identify any consequences of this goal that you don't like, take the time to think up ways to get the positive benefits you are getting now, at the same time as achieving your goal.

Choice: Ensure that your goal is stated as an increase of your choices (if you've stated it positively it will be). Notice what new choices you will get once you achieve this goal.

Initiated by Self: Ensure your goal describes what you will do, have or be; not what someone else will. If your goal is about someone else, ask yourself "What could I do that would make it *most* likely that this other person will reach the goal I have for them?" Now make *"What you could do"* your goal; knowing you cannot guarantee it will have specific results for the other person. Rewrite your goal if needed.

First Step: What could you do *today* that starts you on the path to your goal (apart from this exercise)? Write this down.

Your Resources: Identify and write down examples of the following resources you can use to help you reach your goal.
♦ What other goals similar to this (though maybe smaller) have you achieved before? The strategies you used there may be useful here.
♦ Who do you know of who has already achieved this goal? Their strategy may be useful for you.
♦ Who do you know that you can tell about your goal? Who can give you encouragement, support and ideas?
♦ Where can you get more information about achieving your goal?
♦ What time and physical resources (like money, work) will you to put aside to work towards this goal?
♦ What resource states do you have in your personal experience that you could anchor and use to empower you to achieve this outcome (remember chapter 3)?

3. Make a commitment to yourself to use every resource you have, in your action towards this goal. Make sure you take the action you've set for today, and know which actions you'll do next.

4. Set a date not more than a quarter of the way from now to when you'll achieve your goal. This is a review of progress date. Write it in your diary or on a calendar. At that time you'll:
♦ Check if you've achieved your goal.
♦ Check which actions are working, which to change or add.
♦ Check if your goal is still appropriate; otherwise reuse this process.
♦ Congratulate yourself on any progress and on any learnings. *Every* action has results.
♦ Set the next review date.

Chapter 7:
The Secret to Supportive Relationships

Rapport: Synchronising at the Level of the Brain

Everything you hope to achieve in your relationships will depend on what NLP calls the "rapport" between you and your family and friends. Rapport is the feeling of shared understanding, trust and cooperation that close friends develop. It begins in the brain itself.

Here is a simple experiment which explains how our brain makes sense of the world.

Think of a fresh lemon. Imagine one in front of you now, and feel what it feels like as you pick it up. Take a knife and cut a slice off the lemon, and hear the slight sound as the juice squirts out. Smell the lemon as you lift the slice to your mouth and take a bite of the slice. Taste the sharp taste of the fruit.

If you actually imagined doing that, you mouth is now salivating. Why? Because your brain followed your instructions and thought about, saw, heard, felt, smelled and tasted the lemon. Your brain treated the imaginary lemon as if it was real, and your glands prepared saliva to digest it. In order to think about the lemon, your brain actually experienced it. As an adult, you have enough "reality checking ability" to interrupt the process (by thinking about something else). Your young child doesn't.

About ten years ago, Italian scientists studying the brain made an interesting discovery. They were observing which neurons (nerve cells) fire as a person lifts their arm to pick up a book. They then noticed that some of these neurons also fired when the person watched someone else lift their arm to pick up the book. These neurons are called mirror neurons because they produce a "mirror-like" reflection of what we see, inside our brain. Really, this is the same process as thinking about an imaginary lemon and salivating. In order to understand what is happening when the other person lifts their arm, the observer's brain creates the feeling of what is happening, inside the observer's body.

The mirror neurons pay special attention to movements, facial expressions and sounds made by other human beings, because these are extremely important to us as humans. When I see someone else smiling, or hear them laughing, I get the feeling inside me. My mouth automatically smiles.

Our ability to learn complex social skills - everything from smiling at appropriate times to speaking a language – depends on the mirror neurons. The feeling of shared understanding, of "closeness" to another human being, also depends on them. This feeling is called "rapport" in NLP. You have had that experience many times. A time when you feel as if you could complete the sentences that a friend is saying, before they actually say the words. A time when you were enjoying being with someone else and you just knew that they were enjoying that too. When two people have this feeling, they are more open to each other's ideas and suggestions. They cooperate better.

Seattle's Washington University researchers John and Julie Gottman have done in depth research on more than a thousand married couples over the last thirty years. This research has shown, for example, that in general the objective amount of similarity between the couples personalities and even the number of arguments between the couple are both irrelevant to marital happiness. The Gottmans' research shows that what makes the difference is the level of *rapport*. Couples who stay together actually feel closer, and feel more alike, because they stay in rapport. When they are videotaped, they actually adjust their bodies to experience what the other person is experiencing. They breathe in time with each other, sit in similar positions, use similar voice tonality, and even their heart rates match. By observing any 5 minutes of conversation between a couple, and watching for these indications of rapport, it is possible to predict which marriages will work and which will not. That means that everything else you learn about communication and about creating resilient relationships depends on this one factor first of all!

In separate research, William Condon has carefully studied videotapes of family conversations, confirming this pattern. He found that in a conversations in a happy family, movements such as a smile or a head nod are involuntarily matched by the other person within 1/15 of a second. Within minutes of beginning the conversation, the volume, pitch and speech rate (number of sounds per minute) of the peoples voices match each other and they are breathing in time with each other.

How To Create Rapport

The most exciting thing to come out of all this research is the knowledge that when the feeling of rapport is not present, we can choose to create it. By matching the body positions, movements, voice qualities and even the breathing of another person, you can actually create the quality that research shows is central to all close family relationships. With this one skill you will maximise the chances that your marriage or partnership will survive, create a feeling of safety and love for your child, and learn the social skills that help you survive crisis.

And amazingly, you are already an unconscious expert at this! You have been doing it unconsciously in most relationships since before you were born. All we need to do now is show you how to do it consciously, so you can choose to create rapport when you need it most. It's like speaking your native language. You learned to do it naturally in your first years of life. By studying it now, you can learn to speak it even more skilfully and explain your ideas clearly when it is most important to you.

Despite the fact that many people have spent their whole life searching for it, rapport is *easy* to create. There's only one thing you need to do: make your behaviours similar in form to those of the person you're with. When your behaviours "pace" or "match" theirs, what you say will make sense in their map of the world. They'll actually be willing, at a very deep level, to accept your suggestions and follow your lead. This process is so powerful, that before you read on I want you to make a commitment to yourself now that you will only use these skills ethically, for the mutual benefit of yourself and those you're with.

Nonverbal Qualities You Can Match

There are a number of things you can match in a person's behaviour to create rapport.

1) **Voice**. You can match the volume (loudness), speed, tone (high or low), and timbre (individual quality, like rough or soft) of the voice when speaking with someone. This is especially important when on the phone. As a phone counsellor, I've had the experience of realising that unless I can quickly establish rapport, a caller may be about to hang up and commit suicide. How can I convey to them, in just a few words, that I know what it's like in their world? One thing's for sure: if they speak slow and quiet, I don't want to shout back in a fast "bouncy" voice. I use exactly the same quality of voice they have, even though my words may be disagreeing with what they've said.

Secondly, I listen carefully to the words the person uses, and use similar wording. I'll discuss this aspect of rapport a lot more in the chapter on sensory intelligences. If the other person talks about how gloomy life is, I talk about their search for the light at the end of the tunnel. If they talk about how bogged down they've been, I explore how they can loosen things up and break free.

2) **Eye movements.** Ever seen two people talking and both staring at the same spot on the ground? They're in rapport. Using your eyes to gesture similarly to the person you're with will help you to access the same kind of inner experience they have. Use a similar level of eye contact to what they feel comfortable with. This varies culturally. In Pacific cultures, for example, eye contact is used far less than in European cultures.

3) **Gestures and general body position**. There are two ways to copy someone's body position or gestures. One is to match them; which means that if they cross their left leg over their right leg, you cross your left leg over your right leg. The second way is to "mirror" them. In this case if they cross their left leg over their right leg, you cross your right leg over your left leg. Mirroring makes you look like a mirror image of the other person.

The aim of matching and mirroring isn't to mimic someone. Mimicking usually means exaggerating someone's body language in order to make a joke of it. What you're learning to do is more subtle, and needs to be done in such a way that it doesn't consciously distract the person. Rapport is a natural, unconscious process. You've always used it. You're just learning to use it knowingly. As you do, move one part of your body at a time, rather than suddenly leaping into the same position as the other person. Watch carefully what gestures they make while talking, and then copy these as you speak.

4) **Breathing**. Co-ordinating your breathing with someone else is a very deep way to establish rapport. And yet this too is something you've done many times. When two people sleep together in the same room, their breathing naturally co-ordinates. If you breath in time with someone and then gradually slow your breathing down, they will tend to slow down. Many parents have learned to put their children to sleep using this kind of rapport process. By lying down beside the child and gradually slowing their breathing, they slow down the child's breathing until sleep begins. The secret of success is to begin at the same rate as the child (or at least at one of your breaths to two if theirs). If you start off breathing slow, you'll be so out of rapport the child will simply wake up. People breathe at different rates. If you're copying a fast breather, take smaller "sips" of breath than usual and consider breathing one of your breaths to two of theirs. If you're copying a slow breather, take bigger, deeper breaths.

Because breathing rapport is so deep, there are times when it is inappropriate. You don't usually want to co-ordinate your breathing with that of a person having an asthma attack, for example. So what can you do? One answer is to move some other part of your body in time with their breathing; for example swinging your leg back and forward as they breath in and out, or patting a baby on the back in time with the baby's breathing. If you are massaging a baby, you could move your hands in time with the baby's breathing rate.

Sometimes people wonder how you can tell how someone is breathing. It's not always appropriate to stare at the chest! Instead, watch their shoulders moving up and down, or watch their abdomen rise and fall. You can easily see such movement out of the corner of your eye.

An Example Of Using Rapport

The developers of NLP learned the process of rapport building from a rather extraordinary medical doctor, Milton Erickson. Milton Erickson (1901-1980) lived in Phoenix, Arizona and had eight children. As a hypnotherapist, Erickson usually invited his clients to relax into a daydreaming or "trance" state in which they could consider new ways of dealing with their challenges. With children especially, he accomplished this simply by breathing in time with them, and then slowing down his own breathing so that they relaxed with him. One five year old boy noticed this and commented to him "Ebby night my mommy swings me to sweep, but you bweathe me to sleep." ("Every night my mother sings me to sleep; but you breathe me to sleep.")

When Erickson's son Robert was seven years old, he was involved in a traffic accident. Hit by a truck, he suffered skull and other fractures. On his return home from hospital, his parents discovered that he was having nightmares. These began with him moaning, then crying, and then screaming "Oh, oh, it's going to hit me – it's going to hit me!" followed by a sudden collapse into slow almost comatose breathing. He was unable to be woken from these nightmares, which sometimes happened several times in one night. (Erickson, 1980, p 361, p 195-197)

Milton Erickson realised that he could not "fight against" the nightmares, which were being produced unconsciously. He could not explain them away rationally. He needed to make a connection with the dream itself. He needed to establish rapport with the part of Robert's brain that was generating the nightmares. To do that, he sat by Robert's bed while Robert was asleep, and waited, breathing in time with Robert. As the moaning began at the start of the nightmare, Milton began to speak in a similar tone, simply agreeing with what Robert was experiencing. "Something's going to happen – it's going to hurt you bad – it's going to hit you – hurt you – hit you – hurt you awful bad." As Robert's sleeping voice became faster, Milton's also speeded up, and when Robert fell asleep again, Milton stopped talking too.

After repeating this for two nights, Milton wanted to check that he had unconscious rapport with Robert. So he began talking before Robert had the dream, saying the same words in the same voice. This time, Milton's words actually initiated the nightmare. Now, Milton knew that his voice was linked by rapport to Roberts dream-state. Later that night, Milton began the speech again, and as Robert's moaning began, Milton added a simple sentence: "There's another truck on the other side of the street and that one won't hit you. It will just go right by." This, of course, may have been true in the real situation. In any event, Milton wasn't trying to deny what had happened; merely to shift Robert's attention to more pleasant realities. Robert seemed to relax more easily and fall asleep again.

The following night, when Robert had the nightmare, Milton began as before, and added another sentence: "There's a truck coming, and it's too bad that it's going to hit you. You will have to go to the hospital, but that will be alright because you will come home, and you will get all well. And all the other cars and trucks on the road you will see, and you will keep out of their way." This addition now suggests that Robert can trust that he will survive and even that he will learn things from this event.

After repeating this process a few more times, Milton reported that the nightmares stopped altogether and Robert continued to sleep comfortably through the night the rest of his childhood.

Key Concept: Rapport

The feeling of rapport or shared understanding is created by matching unconscious behaviour such as:
- Voice tonality and word choice
- Eye movements.
- Gestures and general body position
- Breathing

Practical Exercises: Day 7

1. Auditory Rapport. The easiest way to practise building rapport is to divide the learning into three simpler sections. Allow about five minutes for each of the three sections. If possible, practise at first with adults who don't know you, so they don't consciously notice the changes in your voice, position and gestures as you match them. Firstly, practise adjusting your voice to be similar to another person's, aiming to use exactly the same tone, speed, loudness, emphasis and timbre (voice quality) as the original person.

2. Visual Rapport. Next, practise matching other people's body position and gestures. Use the same gestures when you speak, as the other person uses while speaking.

3. Kinesthetic Rapport. Now practise breathing in time with someone for a few minutes. It's easier to practice with someone who is not speaking at first. If you breathe in time with someone who is speaking, they are breathing out while they speak, and will take short fast in-breaths every so often. Watch for subtle movements of the shoulders and tummy to detect breathing. Remember that people breathe at different rates. If you're copying a fast breather, take smaller "sips" of breath than usual and consider breathing one of your breaths to two of theirs. If you're copying a slow breather, take bigger, deeper breaths.

Chapter 8:
Relationships That Survive

The survival of close relationships is an important part of how we maintain our resilience. In this chapter I want to review what we know from research about how to create friendships that survive challenging times.

It's no secret that one to one intimate relationships (such as marriage) are more challenging to maintain in the world today. In the United States, for example, between 50% and 67% of first marriages end in divorce, and the percentage is higher for each subsequent marriage and higher for non-marital intimate partnerships. One sad result of this is increased illness. Those of us who are able to stay in an intimate couple (whether we are male or female) will live approximately 4 years longer, making the couples lifestyle one of the most significant life extension interventions known (Gottman and Silver, 1999, p 4). The cost of separation in economic terms is the source of many jokes, but it is also a realistic fact that people who separate, after living together for any length of time, considerably affect their financial future.

The Gottman Revolution In Couples Counselling

Seattle's Washington University researchers and marital therapists John and Julie Gottman have been in the forefront of a revolution in couples work. Their in depth research on more than a thousand couples over the last thirty years has debunked many cherished theories about what makes intimate relationships work. It has shown, for example, that in general the personality characteristics and even the objective degree of similarity between the couple's personality types is irrelevant to marital happiness. Even the number of arguments between the couple does not determine a couple's sense of satisfaction and likelihood of separation. However, in happy couples, each person perceives the other as being basically a functional person (with certain quirks) and basically similar to them. In happy couples, each perceives arguments as useful and manageable expressions of differences. In unhappy relationships, each partner perceives the other as basically flawed and unlike them, and conflicts are experienced as emotionally traumatic (Gottman, 1999, p 19-21).

When couples are videotaped 24 hours a day, the difference between happy couples and unhappy couples is very small – for example it includes happy couples saying approximately 100 more words of positive comment per day (a mere 30 seconds more of positive talking) compared to unhappy couples. But those 30 seconds are crucial (Gottman, 1999, p 59). Furthermore there are subtle differences in the linguistic patterns that successful couples use before, during and after an argument. These differences in linguistic patterns pervade the whole relationship though, not just the arguments. Gottman's researchers have shown that they can accurately predict whether a couple will divorce just by listening to a five minute conversation between the couple, by identifying the specific language patterns used and seeing the specific non-verbal responses they make to each other (Gottman and Silver, 1999, p 3). They can predict whether a couple will be together twelve years later, and do so with 96% accuracy. But these detailed differences are not merely present in arguments. As Gottman says, his research has shown that "successful conflict resolution isn't what makes marriages succeed." (Gottman and Silver, 1999, p 11). The formation of an intimate relationship, Gottman's research shows, is the formation of a whole new culture. It is the quality of the friendship between the couple, as evidenced in their exact verbal and non-verbal communication, which counts, for both men and women.

Gottman says "In my therapy the entire problem-solving process is recast as one of identifying and harmonizing people's basic life dreams. Much of the process of conflict resolution is an exploration in using the marital friendship to help make one another's life dreams come true." (Gottman, 1999, p 184).

Rapport

This research has shown, for example, that in general the objective amount of similarity between the couples personalities and even the number of arguments between the couple are both irrelevant to marital happiness. The Gottmans' research shows that what makes the difference is the level of *rapport*. Couples who stay together actually feel closer, and feel more alike, because they stay in rapport. When they are videotaped, they actually adjust their bodies to experience what the other person is experiencing. They breathe in time with each other, sit in similar positions, use similar voice tonality, and even their heart rates match. By observing any 5 minutes of conversation between a couple, and watching for these indications of rapport, it is possible to predict which marriages will work and which will not. That means that everything else you learn about communication and about creating resilient relationships depends on this one factor first of all! The feeling of rapport or shared understanding is created by matching unconscious behaviour such as:
- Voice tonality and word choice
- Eye movements.
- Gestures and general body position
- Breathing

Practical Exercises: Rapport

1. Auditory Rapport. The easiest way to practise building rapport is to divide the learning into three simpler sections. Allow about five minutes for each of the three sections. If possible, practise at first with adults who don't know you, so they don't consciously notice the changes in your voice, position and gestures as you match them. Firstly, practise adjusting your voice to be similar to another person's, aiming to use exactly the same tone, speed, loudness, emphasis and timbre (voice quality) as the original person.

2. Visual Rapport. Next, practise matching other people's body position and gestures. Use the same gestures when you speak, as the other person uses while speaking.

3. Kinesthetic Rapport. Now practise breathing in time with someone for a few minutes. It's easier to practice with someone who is not speaking at first. If you breathe in time with someone who is speaking, they are breathing out while they speak, and will take short fast in-breaths every so often. Watch for subtle movements of the shoulders and tummy to detect breathing. Remember that people breathe at different rates. If you're copying a fast breather, take smaller "sips" of breath than usual and consider breathing one of your breaths to two of theirs. If you're copying a slow breather, take bigger, deeper breaths.

Clear Problem Ownership

I train instructors of a process for creating cooperative relationships. This process, called Transforming Communication, is explained in more depth in several other books, and here I want to quickly give you the basics.

To begin using the methodology of Transforming Communication in any relationship situation, one simply checks whether at this moment you feel OK or not. You then step into what NLP calls "second position" (imagine being inside the other person) and check whether the other person feels OK or not. There are four possible results to these checks (Gordon, 1974, p38-39):

No Problem Area	Other Person Owns A Problem
I Own A Problem	Both Of Us Own A Problem (Conflict)

1) Neither of us owns a Problem. If both people feel OK, then no problem exists, and the focus of communication can be towards individual and mutual enjoyment. In the situation where neither of us owns a problem, a larger range of ways of speaking will be safe to use (safe in the sense of preserving both of our self esteem, and preserving the relationship). This area where we both feel good offers the most potential for us to grow personally, as each of us has energy free from problem-solving to focus on our goals and on discovery. It is the area where a couple build their "positive emotional bank account" that they may need to draw on in conflict resolution. Instead of thinking that this area doesn't matter, resilient people know that this time where you both feel good is precious. Gottman's research shows that successful couples devote approximately 20 minutes a day to non-problem activities such as:

- Simply responding to each comment or nonverbal communication by their partner. Such communications are called "bids" (kind of like requests for attention or caring) by John Gottman and in a healthy relationship most bids are responded to. Either cooperation or disagreement are indications of a successful bid, but in unhappy couples over 50% of bids are not even detected by the partner (Gottman, 1999, p 201). The person asks for attention and the other person ignores them of even feels annoyed that they asked.
- Making positive and appreciative comments about the relationship. The ratio of positive comments to negative comments in successful relationships is approximately 5 to 1, whereas in unsuccessful relationships it is less than 1 to 1. This is true both in conflict and in everyday interaction (Gottman, 1999, p 59-61). Indeed, Gottman found that in successful relationships, participants (women in particular) tended to monitor and limit the quantity of negative comments by their partners about anything at all. In unsuccessful relationships, they accepted that their partner had a right to be continuously and unproductively angry, unhappy and blaming of both them and others

(Gottman, 1999, p 73-74) . Saying thank you, saying what you like about the other person … is important.

- Discussing each person's values and dreams, and finding shared values and creating shared meanings. Reviewing the history of their relationship and reframing it as a positive story of friendship.
- Sharing meals together, and sharing housework together. Going out together, both for practical purposes such as shopping, and for entertainment.
- Checking in after time apart and each listening to each other's story.

So the first thing to know about preserving your relationship is not "how to resolve conflicts" but how to take advantage of the good times. AND, of course, in every relationship there are times when one or both people don't feel good. If one of the people is in an undesired state, then they "own a problem" in the terms first used by Dr Thomas Gordon (1955). This does not mean that they are "at fault" or "should" change something. It simply means that they are not in their desired state. So now, let's think about the tough times. Possible results 2), 3), and 4) relate to this situation.

2) The other person owns a problem. If I am in a relationship where at this moment I feel okay, and the other person does not (i.e. they are in an undesired or "problem" state), it can be useful to focus my attention on assisting them to reach their desired state. This process occurs when you are listening to your spouse talking about a difficult day, or when you offer to assist your co-worker to learn how to perform a new work task.

Obviously, when the other person is upset, but I feel OK, the focus is on helping them, rather than showing off my ideas and making me feel good. The most effective skills for Helping will be ones that identify the "problem" and the "solution" as existing inside the other person's experience (I will say, for example, "So what you want to change is..." rather than "So what I think you should change is..."). These skills avoid patronising the person by suggesting what they "should" aim for, "should" feel and "should" be able to cope with. These skills include:

- Non-verbal rapport. Gottman's research demonstrates the power of what NLP calls matching and mirroring. Couples who can understand each other actually adjust their bodies to experience what the other person is experiencing. They breathe in time with each other, sit in similar positions, use similar voice tonality, and even their heart rates match (Gottman, 1999, p 27). We discussed this under the heading "Rapport" in the first part of this section.

- Open questions that invite the other person to talk. These usually begin with the words "How…?" and "What…?" rather than the more intrusive "Why…?" or the more leading "Did you…?", "Didn't you…?" and "Don't you…?"
- Reflective listening. This involves restating the person's own experience, opinions and feelings, in words which are similar to theirs e.g. "That was an unpleasant experience then." "You wanted to get a different perspective." In this situation in particular (where the other partner owns a problem), Gottman's research identified that reflective listening was the most powerful response offered by members of successful relationships (Gottman and Silver, 1999, p 87-89.

When you see someone facing a crisis, it can be tempting to rush in and offer emotional help. In a long term study of 1000 elementary school children, Dr Eva Pomerantz of the University of Illinois (2001) found dramatic evidence of the harmful effects of unsolicited parental help and advice. Her research showed that children were more prone to psychological disturbances and to depression in particular when their parents felt more responsible for the children's feelings. The more the parents used what she called "intrusive support", the less competent their children came to feel, and the less happy they became. Parents who did a lot of intrusive support actually ended up controlling what their children could say about their challenges, denying their children's feelings and deepening any feelings of inadequacy that were there.

Michigan State University management professor Russell Johnson studied the differential effects of two types of help in the workplace, and found the same pattern with adults. He compared unsolicited advice (what he called proactive advice) with solicited advice, where the person asked for help (what he called reactive advice). Only reactive advice was usually appreciated, acted on and enhanced the relationship. Unsolicited advice increases perceived power by the adviser, but does not actually help, and actually lowers the self-esteem of the helpee. Also, it is often ill-informed: "What we found was that on the helper side, when people engage in proactive help, they often don't have a clear understanding of recipients' problems and issues, thus they receive less gratitude for it," notes Johnson. (Lee et alis, 2019, p. 197–213)

Reflective listening is the verbal part of rapport, and avoids the helper rushing into intrusive support. To reflective listen, you simply restate the basic idea that the person has said to you. In a series of studies from the 1950s, Fred Fiedler (1951) showed that successful helpers from a number of different schools of therapy tended to use reflective listening more than any other way of talking. This marked them out from unsuccessful therapists so much that what they said had more in common with other effective therapists than with others in their own school of therapy. Five decades of research has tended to support Fiedler's conclusion (Lambert and Bergin, 1994, p 181).

Reflective listening really makes sure that you listen. New students sometimes say "I always thought I was listening, but when I have to say it back I realise it's actually hard work". It is, at first. When people are first learning a new skill, it can feel like work, and it may also sound less natural. With practice, you'll integrate reflective listening into your natural way of talking. Once that happens, you won't have to think out every response, and – most of the time – no one will even notice you're using a new process. You can then simply enjoy being fascinated by what the person is saying to you. Reflective listening itself doesn't require a lot of effort. You don't have to think up the solutions. You don't have to find smart questions to lead the conversation the right way. Actually, the main mistake learners make when helping is to work too hard.

3) I own a problem. Now let's think about the opposite situation, where I am not happy; where I want something to change. If I am in a relationship where at this moment the other person feels okay, and I do not (i.e. I am in an undesired or "problem" state), it can be useful to focus my attention on finding a way for me to reach my desired state. Remember, to say I "own a problem" doesn't mean its my fault, or that I should be the one to fix it…. It just means that the solution needs to work for ME. This process of fixing my problem could be called Problem Solving. If my problem is related to or about the other person (if I'm upset or angry or hurt "about something they did", for example) then this process of problem solving is called Assertion. For example, I own a problem where I'm frustrated about my spouse's failure to wash the dishes, or where I'm resentful that I ended up doing extra work when my partner didn't arrive home on time. The most effective first skill for Assertion will be one that identifies the "problem" as existing inside my own experience ("What I want to change is..." rather than "So what you might want to do is..."). This skill is called an "I message" (Gordon, 1974, 139-145). In a conflict, a clear I message identifies:

- the sensory specific behaviour that is the subject of the concern (what I saw, heard and touched in the real world, before I decided to label it as not OK),
- the internal state (emotion) which I have generated in response to this behaviour (how I feel),
- any sensory specific effects on me of that behaviour.. (things I have to do differently as a result of the events)

An example of the format for an I message would be "When...[sensory specific behaviour], I feel...[congruent description of my internal state] and the effect on me is... [sensory specific effects of the behaviour]". This structure avoids insulting or blaming the other person, and avoids patronising them by telling them what they "should" do. By not suggesting one specific solution, it leaves the process of generating solutions until the other person's situation has been heard and can be taken into account (as in examples below).

In the last section we learned how to help the other person when they were upset. Helping skills by themselves will be ineffective in the area where I own a problem, suggesting to the other person that it's up to them what solution is reached.

In his research on couples, American psychologist John Gottman found evidence again and again that the first thing someone says in a disagreement is crucial. He notes about couples "The bottom-line rule is that, before you ask your partner to change the way he or she drives, eats or makes love, you must make your partner feel that you are understanding. If either (or both) of you feels judged, misunderstood, or rejected by the other, you will not be able to manage the challenges in your marriage. This holds for big s and small ones...There's a big difference between "You are such a lousy driver. Would you please slow down before you kill us?" and "I know how much you enjoy driving fast. But it makes me really nervous when you go over the speed limit. Could you please slow down?" Maybe that second approach takes a bit longer. But that extra time is worth it since it is the only approach that works." (Gottman and Silver, 1999, p 149).

Gottman recorded hundreds of thousands of hours of marital conflicts. He found that in 96% of cases, the emotional tone of the first one minute of a conflict could predict exactly how that conflict would go overall, and also predict whether the couple's marriage would survive. The first statement in a conflict will decide what the entire conflict turns out like (Gottman, 1999, p 41). It is worth thinking carefully about the precise wording of your first sentence when you ask someone to change. The choice of those few little words will decide whether your relationship survives or not. The most important aim of your first sentence is not to win the argument, it is to keep rapport so that you can get what you want **and** preserve a cooperative relationship with the other person.

Generally, it is important to understand that I messages are a gentle start-up to a discussion that can resolve your problem, rather than intended to be a "final word" that solves the problem. Sometimes, of course, I will say an I message and the other person will say "Wow; I didn't know you had that problem. I will do something different. Thanks for telling me." But not always! Often when you send an I message you will discover that the other person is not happy to change because they themselves have some other opinion or some other problem.

4) We both own a problem. This situation implies that some combination of skills will be useful (So what you want is... and what I want is...). Where we both own a problem in response to the same event, then this situation is a "Conflict". This doesn't mean that we are necessarily opposed to each other, or that one of us must win and one lose. It simply means that we both are upset, angry, hurt etc. about related issues (e.g. I think we should spend more time together and the other person wants more space. I want to use the family car tomorrow and so does my partner) Such situations benefit from a combination of the helping and assertive skills, as well as from specific conflict resolution skills (including win-win conflict resolution, consulting and modelling).

John Gottman's research reveals that successful couples differ not merely in their handling of conflicts, but in their handling of each of these four Problem Ownership areas. That means that effective coaching of couples needs to teach the couple to respond differently in each of the four areas also (Gottman, 1999, p 59-61).

Varying Results of Effectively Raising A Concern

The situation would be very easy if problem ownership stayed constant throughout any conversation. If this was the case, in the "no-problem" situation, a conversation would involve simply exploring positive states and outcomes together. In the "other owns a problem" situation, a conversation would involve simply pacing the other person's dilemma, assisting the other person to clarify what their outcome is, and guiding them through processes to assist change towards that. In the "I own a problem" situation, a conversation would involve simply asserting my position and identifying the changes I want.

In real life, it is more useful if I continuously monitor the changing internal states of myself and the other person, and adjust my language use to best represent the shifts of problem ownership, many of which are of course a result of my own previous communications. For example, in the midst of helping my partner solve her or his problem, I may discover that I myself am uncomfortable with the way my partner insists that I listen to complaints about what goes wrong, and does not shift to an outcome (solution focused) frame. From using Helping skills ("So for you the problem is..." and "So what you want is...") I would then shift to using Assertive skills ("One thing I'm finding frustrating about the way you're talking is..." and "I'd find it easier to help if...").

Most particularly, once I have used an Assertive skill, a common outcome is for my partner to shift into the problem state themselves (to feel uncomfortable in response to what I said). When a person hears my I message "I resented the way you didn't get that report to me on time as we'd arranged. It involved me in a lot of extra work" it is rare for them to respond with congruent joy and enthusiasm to improve next time. If you think of times when someone has, however skilfully, asserted themselves with you in this way, you'll notice that you're more likely to experience feelings of embarrassment, discomfort, hurt, annoyance, and self-protective responses. That is to say, you're more likely to own a problem about the message, and possibly about the issue. Of course, the person who hears this kind of message may then become silent, argue back, deny the problem and so on.

If I've used an I message (Assertion skill) and the other person owns a problem about that, the next step to getting my problem solved will be to shift back from Assertion, and help them solve their own problem. To do this, I simply use reflective listening (a Helping language pattern), to pace their concern (e.g. "You think I'm over-reacting..."). As NLP points out, there is no resistance, only a lack of rapport. Once the other person feels fully heard in their own problem state (evidenced usually by a nod of the head), then it becomes possible to restate my I message taking into account their comment. As they have now been heard, their "emotional temperature" is reduced, and they are more able to hear my concern and respond positively to it.

The process of resolving such a situation by alternating between I messages and reflective listening is called the two step" in Transforming Communication because it is like a dance. Here's how it might sound in practice, in a discussion where Joan is using the model in a concern with her work colleague, Frank (notice that if Frank knew the model, the process would be even more fluent, but Joan can use the model regardless of this):

Joan: Frank, I have a problem I'd like to discuss. You arrived home an hour later than expected a couple of times last week and I didn't get the time to myself in the evening that I was hoping for, and I guess I feel a bit resentful about spending that much of my day child-minding. [Joan "owns" a problem: she is the one who is concerned about what has happened, so she uses an I message. Frank is feeling Okay, so initially he doesn't own a problem.]
Frank: [sighs] Lighten up Joan. I had a busy day; that's all.

Joan: You think I'm over-reacting, and you had a lot of extra stuff to do. [Frank responds indicating that he owns a problem, so Joan does the Two Step and reflective listens him.]

Frank: [nods] Sure. And it's no big deal.

Joan: Well, I still want to know that I have time to myself to do the things that I really want to do. My day is long too. [Frank's nod indicates he feels paced/understood, so Joan Two Steps and restates her I message.]

Frank: Look, I guess I just forgot how important this can be to you. I'll be more careful. How about, if I do arrive late in future, I could adjust later and give you extra time on the weekend.

Joan: Thanks. I would appreciate your help with that.

Frank: Okay. I just wasn't thinking. Sorry. [Frank is now apologising. As he's still not feeling totally comfortable, Joan again acknowledges his comments before thanking him for changing his approach.]

Joan: Well I'd appreciate sort of knowing that the time for myself is there. Thanks.

This, of course, is a "best case" scenario. There are two other possible outcomes of this discussion, described below. Both are "conflicts".

John Gottman found that such discussions and conflicts occurred in even the best relationships, and that effective couples might get very emotional (even angry) as they talked about such issues, but they avoided certain key destructive behaviours. Those seven core behaviours to avoid (listed by Gottman and Silver, 1999, p 25-46) include:

- Harsh Start-up of the discussion with an angrily stated "You message"
- Criticism of the person as a person rather than complaint about their behaviour.
- Contempt of the other person, conveyed nonverbally by raised eyebrows and a sneering facial expression, or verbally by mockery of the person's position, sarcasm and hostile humour. This is the most serious of the seven behaviours, it is the fastest way to predict separation, and it is virtually unseen in successful relationships (Gottman, 1999, p 128)
- Defensiveness, expressed by arguing/blaming back while refusing to acknowledge the other's concern or accept that they have a problem.
- Stonewalling, expressed by simply stopping talking without negotiating, or leaving the room.
- Becoming Emotionally Flooded, as a result of these behaviours, as evidenced by the person being physically over-aroused, with a pulse above 95 beats per minute.

- Not using Repair Attempts and Self-nurturing behaviours, e.g. to call a halt for time to calm down, or to apologise and ask to start again, as these last patterns occur.

Three Types Of Conflict

The Two Step process will lead to one of three outcomes. Depending on which outcome occurs, you can easily identify which steps to take next to most effectively resolve the conflict.

Outcome 1) Misunderstanding. The Two Step process itself resolves the conflict (as above). Such conflict could be considered a simple miscommunication. In the example above, for instance, once Frank has clearly heard what Joan's problem is (which is assisted by her use of I messages and reflective listening) the problem is solved. No further action may be needed.

Outcome 2) Conflict of Needs. As a result of the Two Step process, it becomes clear that both people have a concrete problem. Both people can understand that the other person has a problem, though they are reluctant to solve the other person's problem as this would leave them with their own difficulty. Thomas Gordon calls this a Conflict of Needs. In NLP terms it is a conflict which both parties have agreed to keep at the neurological level of environment, behaviour or capability (their values and sense of identity are not a subject of discussion, only how and where they do what). John Gottman calls this a "Solvable Conflict" and recommends developing solutions which honour both parties "dreams" in the conflict. In such a situation, Gordon recommends the skilled use of his 6 step win-win conflict resolution model (Gordon, 1974, p217-234). Gordon's six steps are:

1. Identify the problem in terms of two sets of needs, rather than two conflicting solutions. Needs are more general descriptions than solutions ("How will you know that this problem is solved?" or "If you get this solution, what do you get through that, that is even more important?" rather than "What specific way would you suggest to solve this problem right now?"). Gottman describes this as discovering what the "dreams" behind the stated solution are.
2. Brainstorm potential solutions which could meet both sets of needs/outcomes/dreams.
3. Evaluate the ability of these proposed solutions to meet both sets of needs.
4. Choose a solution, or several solutions to put into action.
5. Act
6. Evaluate the results.

An example would be if the conversation between Frank and Joan went like this:

Joan: Frank, I have a problem I'd like to discuss. You arrived home an hour later than expected a couple of times last week and I didn't get the time to myself in the evening that I was hoping for, and I guess I feel a bit resentful about spending that much of my day child-minding. [Joan "owns" a problem: she is the one who is concerned about what has happened, so she uses an I message. Frank is feeling Okay, so initially he doesn't own a problem.]
Frank: [sighs] Lighten up Joan. I had a busy day; that's all.
Joan: You think I'm over-reacting, and you had a lot of extra stuff to do. [Frank responds indicating that he owns a problem, so Joan does the Two Step and reflective listens him.]
Frank: [nods] Sure. And if I come home without completing that stuff, I'll end up in rouble at work.
Joan: So you want to make sure you get the things done at work that are your responsibility. Well, I still want to know that I have time to myself to do the things that I really want to do. My day is long too. Maybe we can find a way to meet both those concerns. [Frank now understands that Joan has a concrete problem, as his nod indicates, but if he agreed to help her, he'd have a problem of his own (trying to guess what issues were serious enough for her). This is what Thomas Gordon calls a Conflict of Needs and John Gottman calls a solvable problem. Joan sums up the two sets of needs/outcomes, and invites Frank to begin win-win conflict resolution to identify a solution which will meet both sets of needs/outcomes.]
Frank. [nods] Yeah. I guess I could adjust later and give you extra time on the weekend if I get home late in the week.
Joan: Thanks. That would work for me too. I would appreciate your help with that.
Frank: Okay. Let's do that.

We see this win-win approach in the work of many religious teachers through history. The Christian apostle Paul advocates this win-win approach and suggests how to use it even when society expects one person to win and one to lose. He emphasised that those with less power should "obey" those with more power (not because they are in power, but out of love of God), but only in the same way as those with more power should respect the rights of those they "control". He then emphasises that in God's eyes, there is no power difference at all. He begins with "Slaves, be obedient to those who are your earthly masters…. Rendering service with a good will as to the Lord and not to men." And then follows with "Masters do the same to them and forbear threatening, knowing that he who is both their master and yours is in heaven, and there is no partiality with him." (Ephesians, 6.5, 6.9). He starts with "Children obey your parents in the Lord" and then adds "Fathers do not provoke your children to anger." (Ephesians, 6.1, 6.4). These comments are repeated (eg Colossians 3.18-4.1) in the same careful form each time. Paul restates the equality of all, for example saying "There is neither Jew nor Greek, there is neither slave nor free, there is neither male nor female; for you are all one in Christ Jesus." (Galations, 3.28). He also repeatedly emphasises that one person cannot pass judgement on another, for example in saying "Therefore you have no excuse, O man, whoever you are, when you judge another; for in passing judgement upon him you condemn yourself, because you, the judge, are doing the very same things." (Romans, 2.1)

Outcome 3) Conflict of Values. As a result of the Two Step process, it becomes clear that at least one person believes that the conflict involves their deeper beliefs, values or sense of identity. In Robert Dilts' NLP model these are disagreements at a higher neurological level (Dilts, 1993, p 55-56). Such a person will be reluctant to engage in the sort of conflict resolution demonstrated above because their values are "non-negotiable". Put another way, Person A believes that Person B is trying to change Person A's values/identity, which Person A considers is really "none of Person B's business". This is what Thomas Gordon calls a "Values Conflict" (Gordon, 1974, p283-306). Note that in this situation it is less likely that a satisfactory solution will be reached in one session.

John Gottman found that 69% of all relationship conflicts were in this category, in both successful and unsuccessful relationships (Gottman and Silver, 1999, p 130). Gottman calls these conflicts "unsolvable problems", where the partners' basic dreams are in conflict. He doesn't mean that nothing can be done about such conflicts; simply that they cannot be resolved in a session of "problem-solving" talk. In fact, he notes that successful couples learn to respect and honour each other's differing values, and accept that the difference will continue for some time.

Thomas Gordon also recommends that many values conflicts are best dealt with by learning to live with the difference, or to altering the relationship so that the other person's values do not clash so frequently with theirs. Skills that are recommended by Thomas Gordon for actually influencing others values include values consulting, and modelling. Modelling involves demonstrating, in one's own behaviour, the effectiveness of one's values. Values consulting is a skilled linguistic influencing process which requires (Gordon, 1974, p294-297):

1. Ensuring you have been "hired" as a consultant (that the other person agrees to listen).
2. Preparing your case, especially researching any relevant information.
3. Sharing your expertise and opinions in simple I message form ("I believe...") and then stepping back to reflective listen the other's opinion.
4. Leaving the other to make up their own mind, rather than attempting to force a new value. People rarely change values in direct interaction with someone who shares the opposing value. It is more common for them to change at a later time, having been left in a positive state, to choose.

If you attempted to resolve Conflicts of Values as if they were Conflicts of Needs, it could well lead to disillusionment with the conflict resolution process, and the belief that "some people just cannot be engaged in a win-win conflict resolution way". Here's how the conversation between Frank and Joan might go if it was a Conflict of Values:

Joan: Frank, I have a problem I'd like to discuss. You arrived home an hour later than expected a couple of times last week and I didn't get the time to myself in the evening that I was hoping for, and I guess I feel a bit resentful about spending that much of my day child-minding. [Joan "owns" a problem: she is the one who is concerned about what has happened, so she uses an I message. Frank is feeling Okay, so initially he doesn't own a problem.]

Frank: [sighs] Lighten up Joan. I had a busy day; that's all.

Joan: You think I'm over-reacting, and you had a lot of extra stuff to do. [Frank responds indicating that he owns a problem, so Joan does the Two Step and reflective listens him.]

Frank: [nods] Sure. I mean, that's my life. My work is also important to me. I don't really feel comfortable negotiating that with you. [Frank identifies a difference in values about the issue]

Joan: So you see that as your life to decide about. Well, I have a different way of thinking about that particular part of it – the timing piece. I'd like to discuss it some more some time. Would you be willing to hear my thoughts about that? [Joan reflective listens Frank's value and identifies the difference.]

Frank: [sighs] Maybe.... Yeah, I guess so. I don't want to get into a heavy discussion about it now though.

Joan: Great. How about the kids are out on Saturday: maybe we could put aside half an hour to clarify our approaches with each other. [Joan arranges to meet with Frank at a time that is easier for him to discuss their values difference. There, she will continue to use reflective listening and I messages to advocate her value, acting as what Thomas Gordon calls a "Values Consultant", and modelling her values.]

Frank: Okay; that'll work.

The Two Step: Three Results Of I Messages

Here on the next page is another example, shown graphically. Imagine that Jane is a teenager who gets up late in the morning. Her father, Jack,finds that this results in him having less time to tidy up before he leaves for work.He decides to send an I message to explain his problem. In the diagrams, when Jack sends his I message, we will have him symbolically move out of rapport by stepping down the page. When Jane feels understood as a result of Jack's reflecting, we will have her move down the page back into rapport. This is a kind of "dance" that I call the "Two Step".

1. Jane agrees congruently to change to solve Jack's problem.

2. Jane agrees her action affects Jack, but has her own problem (Conflict).

3. Jane considers this matter to be "none of Jack's business". Jane is thus not willing to negotiate the issue. (This is a Conflict of Values)

A 4th Possibility?

In some cultures (Japan and New Zealand are examples) conflict is avoided and the other person may not be willing to explain their challenge, and will hide their situation. This is far less common in European cultures. While the other can understand that their behaviour concretely affects you, they are not willing to change because change would create a challenge for them, **and** also they are not comfortable explaining this. The result is that the other superficially agrees, but fails to change their behaviour. This needs a little more care to find out what the other person's needs actually are so you can begin to think up solutions that will meet them and motivate the person to cooperate. (Hidden Conflict of Needs)

Any of these three outcomes is a successful result of sending the I message and reflective listening.

To summarise:

No Problem area: Build positive experiences.	OtherPersonOwns A Problem: Use Reflective listening.
I Own A Problem: Use sensory specific I messages and reflective listen to the response.	Both Of Us Own A Problem (Conflict). Use the win-win method, or in values conflicts use Consulting and Modelling

Key Concept: Problem Ownership

Getting clear who is happy and who is not happy is the first step to knowing how to resolve challenges. Getting clear who "owns the problem" in this sense enables you to choose which skills will be most useful. Intrusive "help" such as solution giving, judgements, denying, and interrogating actually confuses who owns the challenge and blocks the other person from finding solutions that will work for them.

Key Concept: Reflective Listening

The most powerful skill to help someone else resolve their own challenge is reflective listening. To summarise, reflective listening has three steps:
1. Ask yourself what the basic meaning of the person's message was.
2. Put this into a brief statement and say this back, in words that can be understood by the person.
3. Check the person's response to find out whether you understood.

Key Concept: I Messages

When you are not happy with another person's behaviour, you can send an I message which includes:
• Sensory specific description of the behaviour you are unhappy with "When you do…."
• Sensory specific description of any concrete effects on you, that your child would agree you do actually need to cope with. "The result of what happened is…."
• One word description of the feeling state you experienced "I felt…"
You can use reflective listening to check your understanding of the person's response, to bring them back into rapport with you so they can hear what you said, and to check whether;
• The issue is solved by the Two step process of I message and reflective listening

- You have a conflict of needs where other is reluctant to change because they will have a challenge themselves if they do what you ask.
- You have a conflict of values where the other doesn't think this situation concretely affects you and considers this "their own business".

Key Concept: Win-Win Conflict Resolution

In a conflict of needs each person can understand that the other person has a challenge, and is concretely affected by the situation they disagree about. In this case, the challenge is that each person realises that if they change what they do, to help the other person, then they themselves may lose something. This can be solved in a way that works for both people, with a simple but carefully guided discussion process called win-win conflict resolution:

1. "Reframe" the situation as a challenge to be co-operatively solved.
2. Define each person's basic need, intention or outcome (what prompted their actions).
3. Think up solutions which meet both sets of basic outcomes.
4. Evaluate these solutions to check how well they meet both sets of outcomes.
5. Agree on the best solutions.
6. Plan and act on the agreed solutions.
7. Check how the solutions are working.

Key Concept: Values Influencing

To influence another person's values, rather than simply to change their behaviour by coercion:
1. Check what values you share with the person and build rapport with them around those shared values.
2. Check that your behaviour models the value you want the person to have.
3. Know your facts about the issue you are discussing
4. Ask permission to send a consulting I message (get hired)
5. Send the message, including:
- A sensory specific description of the behaviour you are unhappy with "When you do…."
- A one word description of the feeling state you experienced "I feel…"
- A sensory specific description of any concrete effects on the other, which they might agree they do actually need to cope with. "The result for you from what happened could be…."
- Reflective listening the other's response (The Two Step) "So the way you think of it…"
6. Leave the other to decide

Practical Exercises Day 8:

A) Problem Ownership. Read each situation below. If you think that in the situation as described *so far,* the other person/s own a challenge (are upset, unhappy, not getting their needs met etc.) write an "O" for "Other owns a challenge". If you feel that faced with the behaviour described you would own a challenge, write an "I" for "I own a challenge". If both are happy write an "X"

1. The person who shares your workspace plays a radio at a high volume, making it difficult for you to concentrate.
2. A colleague tells you she is worried about failing an important staff evaluation.
3. Your family often have political debates, such as discussing whether Ronald Reagan was a good or bad economist.
4. Your partner expresses disapproval of your taking a training course.
5. A repair shop has failed to meet three consecutive promises to have your car ready.
6. A worker in your department complains that her responsibility level isn't challenging enough.
7. Your partner looks increasingly worried and tense and tells you they "can't cope with it all."
8. One of your family members is increasingly late getting the dishes washed, and you end up waiting to be able to use the bench space.
9. Your child fails to turn up on time for a dental appointment that you must pay for anyway.
10. A lot of your work time is spent willingly giving advice to less experienced staff.

B) Reflective Listening. Read each of the following statements. Write down a word for the feeling state you think the other might be experiencing and expressing. Then write a sentence which you could say back to the person which acknowledges these feelings (reflective listening).

1. Why did grandma have to die *this* year? It's such a mess.
2. I don't want to show my face when dad gets home tonight. I was going to show him my report card, and I can just see the look on his face when he finds I messed up maths.
3. Can you just go over this with me for a minute. I'm really in a stew.
4. I wish you would tell me how I'm doing more often. I always wonder if I'm making a major mistake, and everyone's so quiet about it.
5. Do you think it's fair the way Bill leaves all this mess around like this?

6. Well, wouldn't you do the same thing if you stood in my shoes? What else could I do?

7. I'm really sick of all the noise around here. I can't hear myself think with everyone crashing around all afternoon!

C)Construct an I Message

1) Choose a situation you have recently experienced where you would have liked to confront the other person about the challenge you experienced with their behaviour. Ideally choose a situation which you are likely to experience yourself in again at some future time. Write down a description of the other's BEHAVIOUR without using blaming language (e.g., avoid "when you are so inconsiderate..." or "when you never...." or "when you selfishly..."). Be sensory specific (i.e. describe what you could see, hear or touch.

2) Then list the actual concrete EFFECTS that this behaviour has for you (if there aren't any; if you feel not accepting of the behaviour but can't see how it concretely affects you, this is possibly a conflict of values. Keep that situation in mind, but choose another for this exercise).

3) Thirdly write down how you FEEL about the behaviour and the effects it has for.

4) After listing the three parts, write out a complete I Message combining all three. Avoid adding a solution or you message.

5) What is the person likely to say when you send the I message? Write down what you would say to reflective listen that reply.

6) Check whether the situation is likely to be a) Solved b) A Conflict of Needs or c) A Conflict of values.

Chapter 9:
Helping Someone In Crisis

Each Crisis Has Three Stages

People often imagine a crisis as a single event. It never is. After the earthquake there are aftershocks. In the case of the 2010-2011 earthquakes in my home town of Christchurch, the aftershock was the biggest killer as it happened to have its epicentre nearer the city. People justifiably were in panic with every shake after that. In 2001, my life partner died. This was a dramatic personal crisis, and of course there was a single event where she stopped breathing. However, over the next few months there were many other events, as big as making decisions about selling a house, as small as realising that there was no-one in the world who now shared all those movies we had watched and discussed together.

Understanding this reality allows you to be gentler with yourself after a crisis. If you are in the situation of trying to help someone else, it also reminds you that helping them depends on knowing where they are in the three stages of crisis: beginning, recovery or long term change. It is a very different situation to catch someone immediately after they have been told bad news, or immediately after a motor vehicle accident; compared to catching them a week later.

In the brain the stages are clear: the first stage of crisis is occurring while the experience is first being laid down in the hippocampus (temporary memory storage area) and while it may have highest priority in the amygdala (which truly functions at that time like a panic alarm system). The second stage of crisis occurs over the next few weeks as the memory is reconsolidated to the cortex (longer term storage) and made sense of by connecting it to all similar memories. At this time the amygdala is hopefully reassessing the level of danger, and even identifying opportunities for growth. The third stage occurs from that time on, as the person adjusts long term to a different reality, and hopefully becomes able to sleep, eat, exercise, and make effective choices again in the new situation they find themselves in.

In this chapter, I overview how to help in the first two stages. In the next chapter we look at how to end longer term challenges and deeper emotional distress. The suggestions in this chapter could be used with study by a lay person. However extreme traumatic responses should of course be dealt with by someone well trained in the methods summarised in the next chapter also.

Helping in the Beginning: "The Worst Is Over"

How do you help someone who is right in the immediate crisis situation? They have just survived an earthquake or a shooting incident, just been told they are fired from their job or have an untreatable illness. The experience is not even rated by their amygdala and not even stored as a separate unit by the hippocampus. They don't even know what is happening fully yet. You are there in real time, rather than reviewing it the next day or the next year.

Just telling them "It will be OK." or "Just hang in there." sounds both clichéd and phoney. But the fear of not knowing what to say and do in this situation keeps many helpers from committing themselves to go into such situations. Actually, you have learned everything you need to know to respond already, but we need to focus it into an easily remembered and utilised algorithm.

That is what Judith Acosta and Judith Simon Prager have done (2002). Their methodology is taught to police, firefighters, medical emergency personnel, psychiatric nurses, employee assistance programs and other first responders. It is actually an application of the process that Milton Erickson used with his son Robert, described in the previous chapter on reframing. Here, I am going to simplify it even further into 4 steps:

1. Deliver and arrange practical help such as first aid and an ambulance.
2. Build rapport and use realistic empathic comments.
3. Shift their attention to helping themselves and focusing on comfort.
4. Use direct hypnotic suggestions that recovery is beginning.

And a mnemonic - ARCS: Aid, Rapport, Comfort, Suggestions

Aid: Deliver and arrange practical help (This is mostly for medical crises)
- If anything is obstructing their breathing, unblock the airway (e.g. using the Heimlich manoeuvre – abdominal thrusts). Ensure the person is moved safe from obvious sources of further injury.
- If there is a loss of pulse or breathing, deliver CPR (breathe mouth to mouth with the person lying on their back, head tilted back and use chest compression to restart the heart.
- If there is a medical crisis, and emergency services are reachable by phone, call emergency services(911 in USA, 111 in New Zealand etc.) and give them the details.**Arrange** to get the person to medical help if needed, by ambulance or failing that in a car.
- Use other first aid as per the first aid manuals. For example use direct pressure to stop arterial bleeding.

Rapport: Build rapport and use realistic empathic comments

- State your intention to help. "I'm [your first name] and I'm going to help you. Will you stay here and relax a little while I help?" Even in an emergency, you need a kind of psychological contract with the person to help them. They need to accept your suggestions and support. Don't assume, ask.
- Create rapport. Physically touch the person calmly, and make eye contact. If you are able to, adjust something such as your nodding to the rhythm of their breathing, and slow it down gently. Acknowledge their fear "I can imagine this has been really scary."

Comfort: Shift their attention

- Say "The worst is over." Research showed this was the most realistic single sentence reassurance helpers could give. Explain it - e.g. In physical injury "Your body is already healing itself, and help is coming." In job loss "Your mind is already processing the news and we can begin planning the most important first things to do."
- Give them a task to do that shifts their attention from the problem to areas of functionality, and lets them feel they are helping too. e.g. "I can see your [body part] needs attention. Can you help me check the rest of your body and tell me how it feels here… and here… and here?" "Can you hold this phone and check if anyone messages me, while I bandage your arm." "Can you write your name here while I talk to this person on the phone."

A significant part of how crisis is distressing to people is the sense that they are completely out of control of the events happening. It is not just that the events "feel bad" but more that the person is dehumanised by not having any sense of participating. Their sense of self is shaken. Asking them to help is an important signal that they are regaining some control, however small. Otherwise the risk is that the help itself is traumatic, removing the last sense of choice.

Suggestions: Use direct hypnotic suggestions that recovery is beginning.

The state of psychological "shock" is a state in which the person does not know how to fully make sense of what has happened. Because of that, your comments are not filtered, as they usually are, by the persons conscious frame. As a result, they tend to accept the information you give them. In this sense they are in a kind of "trance". Acosta and Prager (2002, front) quote from the American Academy of Orthopaedic Surgeons: "During periods of great stress, words that seem immaterial or are uttered in jest might become fixed in the patient's mind and cause untold harm." The reverse, of course, is that simple positive suggestions may cause untold good.

Suggestions are easiest assimilated if you connect them to something that the person already knows is true. You thus "pace" their current experience (walk alongside it) and "lead" to a positive suggestion. The brain is wired so that it responds to "cause and effect" claims. Harvard psychologist Ellen Langer(1989) showed that if her students asked to queue jump at the library photocopier, suggesting that they needed to go ahead in the queue *because* of some reason increased compliance dramatically. If the student said "Excuse me, I have five pages. May I use the Xerox machine?", they were successful 60% of the time, but if they sad "Excuse me, I have five pages. May I use the Xerox machine *because* I have to make some copies?" they were successful 93% of the time. With no logical extra information, the implied connection made it seem that the other person was obligated to agree. It is even more elegant to reverse the sentence and say "As you already agree with this fact … you can now also …." This is why young children don't just ask "Can I have an ice-cream?". They say "It's very hot isn't it …. So can I have an ice-cream?" The parent agrees it is hot, so they feel almost obligated to buy the ice-cream.

In a crisis, this actually just means making simple statements that start with the real experience happening and shift attention to future positive changes. You can connect these positive changes to the real situation by saying "As [real experience happens] … you can [useful shift in attention, thought or belief] : e.g.

- "As you hold my hand you may notice the tingly feeling that lets you know healing is happening, and you can realize that the emergency services are on their way and you can relax."
- "As we have now cleaned up the wound, your body can stop the blood flow here, and you can begin to notice which way to position yourself to feel more comfortable."
- "As we wait for the help to arrive, you can think of a place where it would be nice to be resting right now, perhaps cooling this arm in a nice mountain stream, or relaxing in a warm bath."
- "As you notice sound of my voice, you can adjust your internal voice so that you continue to breathe more calmly and enjoy more sense of being in more charge of what happens next."

Milton Erickson (Rossi ed. 1989, p176-179) used the whole method like this with his young child:
1. *Deliver and arrange practical help.* His 3 year old son Robert fell down the back stairs, split his lip and impacted a tooth into his jaw.

The boy screamed in pain and terror, staring horrified at the blood all over the pavement. Milton arrived and assessed the injury, realising he needed to clean the wound, stop the bleeding and get the child to a clinic where his lip could be stitched.

2. *Build rapport and use realistic empathic comments.* Milton did not need to introduce himself of course. His first comment was "That hurts awful, Robert! That hurts terrible." Robert nodded, crying in terror. "And it will keep right on hurting. And you really wish it would stop hurting."

3. *Shift their attention.* Milton then pointed out "And we don't know if the hurting will stop in one minute, or in two minutes." Robert agreed. This also was very true. Erickson continued, pointing to the blood which had so terrified Robert "That's an awful lot of blood on the pavement…. And is it good strong red blood?" Robert wasn't sure. Milton explained that if it was good strong red blood, it would turn the water pink when they washed his face clean. They went into the bathroom to check. Thus he shifted Robert's attention to the next actions he could take to help.

4. *Use direct hypnotic suggestions.* Later, as they drove to the clinic, Milton began to carry on talking about the stitches Robert would get, just as his older brother Allan and older sister Betty Alice had had. Milton speculated as to whether Robert would be able to get as many stitches as they had been able to get. Robert was very curious about that. Milton essentially said "I can see that your lip needs stitches, and you can be curious about whether you will get as many stitches as your older siblings got."

Remember: ARCS: Aid, Rapport, Comfort, Suggestions

Helping in the Recovery Period: Practical Help In The Next Weeks

Aid: Getting Practical Help First

In the "recovery" period, over the weeks after an initial crisis, the same principles apply if you offer someone help. The sequence is Aid – Rapport – Comfort – Suggestions.

Aid for the real physical problems comes first. Physical actions to provide safety, water, food, community support and eventually electricity and sewage become priorities rather than counselling sessions in the immediate aftermath of disaster. In an earthquake, aftershocks continue to happen for some weeks and alertness about danger is a realistic response. In an individual event such as a medical crisis or a job loss, practical details such as checking insurance, planning for further emergencies, and notifying others are often significant concerns. They come before fancy counselling and "emotional transformation".

Rapport: Get Permission to Help and Show You Understand

In the chapter of "Relationships That Survive", I discussed the dangers of "Intrusive support". To restate: When you see someone facing a crisis, it can be tempting to rush in and offer emotional help. Dr Eva Pomerantz of the University of Illinois (2001) studied emotional help given to elementary school children. Michigan State University management professor Russell Johnson(Lee et alia, 2019, p. 197–213) studied help given to office workers by colleagues. Both found conclusively that unsolicited help and advice lowered the self esteem of the person in crisis and made them more prone to chronic problems later. The helper who gave unsolicited advice usually failed to actually check the person's problems and goals. Only advice that was asked for and accepted by the other person had positive results. A major part of any crisis is fending off unrequested advice. When someone is divorcing, suddenly everyone around them thinks they are a relationship expert. When someone has a medical crisis, suddenly everyone around them is a physician with the most advanced alternative medical cures.

This means that in realty the two effective skills for beginning helping are "asking permission", "open questions" and "reflective listening".

Reflective Listening e.g.
- "Looks like this has been a really difficult time."
- "Feels like there are just so many things happening all at once right?"
- "Sounds like it is difficult to know what to do and where to start."

Ask permission e.g.

- "Would you be interested in talking over what to do?"
- "Would it help if you take a few minutes to talk and get clearer about what is happening?"

If the person says no, it is extremely important to respect that. Forcing them to "get help" they don't want is disempowering and may significantly re-traumatise a person.

Open Questions e.g.
These open questions direct the person's attention away from unhelpful questions such as "What if even worse things are going to happen next?" and "Why did this happen to me anyway?" If you have the person's permission, and you notice them focusing on those less helpful questions,

you could take them through the Key Questions Process explained in the chapter on 3 Responses to Crisis.

- "Ideally, how would you like to be able to respond to this uncertainty?"
- "How would you need to respond to feel really pleased about how you had coped with this challenging situation?"
- "What's important to you about how you deal with this?"
- "How can you best respond now to increase your safety?"

Helpful open questions invite the person to set goals and plan, as discussed in the chapter on "Setting Goals That Work". This means focusing down on realistic small goals. For example, in the earthquake situation, a person may appreciate having a plan for dealing with aftershocks (e.g. count to 3, taking breaths, if it's still moving, go to the safest place such as under a table. Know which place to go in every room you are in.) and having an emergency supply with them in their bag at all times.

Comfort: Creating Positive Anchors

The next skills, also explained for your own internal use earlier in the book, are reframing and anchoring. In the chapter on Creating a Resilient State of Mind, we discussed setting positive anchors. In the anxiety after a crisis, it may be harder for the person to remember relaxed times, and you may show them how to physically relax first. One choice is to relax using peripheral vision, relaxing their jaw and spreading their vision out to the side, which triggers an automatic relaxation after a minute or two. Another is adjusting their breathing so they breathe in for two counts, and then breathe out for four counts. This also automatically lowers the blood pressure and creates relaxation physically.

In the next chapter, we look at the really dramatic results that we can offer ourselves and others in the third stage of crisis, when the emotional distress seems, at some level, to go on and on. If you have difficulty creating useful anchors, the two techniques I introduce there are probably the answer you are looking for.

Suggestions: Reframing

In the first weeks after the event, there is often still real physical danger. So, in helping sessions it's really important to accept that some anxiety is normal, and that people also need to be able to relax and rest. It is also important to be able to help the person find ways of accepting their need for rest as a method of ensuring they make the best decisions and stay safe. Here are some examples of "Reframing" in that situation:

Person in crisis "I know that I should try and stop panicking, but I'm afraid that if I get too relaxed I won't be able to respond fast enough if another event happens."
Helper "You wonder if your anxiety is sort of protecting you by helping you stay alert so you can respond quicker."
Person in crisis "Yeah"
Helper "Well I think of it as being like electricity power points in the wall. I know they're dangerous and I need to be alert when I'm round them, but being frightened when I am trying to plug in something doesn't make me safe; it would make me more likely to do something unhelpful. Actually it's being able to be calmly aware that helps me to be most safe."

Person in crisis "I can't stop thinking that this could happen again at any time. How can I ever feel safe again?"
Helper "I agree with you that one of the things we learn from events like this is that the world is not always safe. But what happens out in the world is not what causes us to feel safe or feel unsafe. There are many people who are completely physically safe and have never experienced a physical injury, but who have terrible panic attacks. There are many people who live calmly even though their job, for example cleaning windows on high buildings, involves placing themselves in real physical danger. Feeling safe is something that we do inside. What happens in the world is not predictable and not always in our control. What happens inside us can be changed once we learn how to take charge of our brain. Once we do that we can change the things in the world that can be changed, live comfortably in the uncertainty about those things that we cannot predict or change, and learn to choose wisely which situations are which."

Key Concept: ARCS: Aid, Rapport, Comfort, Suggestions

In the Actual Crisis
Aid: deliver first aid and call help.
Rapport: Say name and ask if you can help. Use rapport and reflecting.
Comfort: "The worst is over", Give them a task.
Suggestions: "As you notice … you can also notice …."

In the Recovery Period
Aid: Provide practical help
Rapport: Reflective listen, Open questions to focus on goals
Comfort: Create anchors, especially using breathing & peripheral vision
Suggestions: Reframe relaxation as part of safety and planning

Practical Exercise Day 9

Rehearse yourself through the ARCS process as if you had come across someone injured in a medium level road accident. Imagine their arm is broken and you have your cell phone ready. Actually say out loud what you plan to say as you help them. For example …

- Aid: As you talk, phone emergency services for an ambulance. Have the person stabilise the injured arm.
- Rapport: "I'm [your first name] and I'm going to help you. Will you stay here and relax a little while I help?" "That must have been really scary."
- Comfort: Shift their attention. E.g. say "The worst is over. Your body is already beginning the healing process" Ask for help "I can see your arm needs attention. Can you help me check the rest of your body and tell me how it feels here… and here… and here?"
- Suggestions: e.g. say "As we wait for the help to arrive, you can think of a place where it would be nice to be resting right now, perhaps cooling this arm in a nice mountain stream, or relaxing in a warm bath."

Chapter 10:
Helping When The Crisis Won't End

The third stage of crisis is the time after the person knows rationally that the events are complete, but their brain doesn't get the message yet. In this section we are learning two powerful, fast interventions to help the brain recode traumatic memories, either soon after the trigger event, or even years after the original trauma. Both of these techniques are aimed at activating the brain's natural reconsolidation process for memories, as discussed in the chapter "How The Brain Reacts to Events".

Since these are processes designed for people with severe traumatic responses such as PTSD, they are not so easy to "run on yourself". Nor are they easy to do without the kind of careful training we offer on our two day Resilience and Trauma Recovery courses. On these courses you become familiar with the underlying structure of an NLP coaching session. As I explain it elsewhere (in our book "Outframes", and in the book "RESOLVE: A New Model of Therapy") this structure can be understood with the acronym RESOLVE:

Resourceful state for the coach
Establish rapport
SPECIFY outcome
Open up client's model of the world
Lead the client to new responses
Verify the change to the client's conscious mind
Ecological exit

RESOLVE: An Example

Here I will use the example of a woman I worked with soon after the Bosnian war, in Sarajevo. I'll call her Fatima.

Resourceful State

Robert Carkhuff showed in the 1950s that a client's success is linked to the personal functioning of their counsellor (Carkhuff and Berenson 1997, pp.5 and pp. 35 2002b, pp. 122–123). Part of the practitioner's resourceful attitude is knowing that, just as in the sports situation where the "coaching" metaphor comes from, change is the client's job and not the coach's. It involves understanding that life itself is the real coach, and the human coach is merely a tour guide. This requires a skill in stepping back, rather than in getting caught up in the client's horror of what happened to them, a skill in trust. I began working with Fatima in Sarajevo by explaining that her panic attacks were simply a result of an "anchored response" and could be quickly changed. Being Resourceful does not mean being confident in the "magic" processes I am using, but being confident in my client's ability to heal and change naturally.

Establish Rapport

As you remember, Rapport is the feeling of shared understanding, trust, and empathy which emerges when you synchronize your verbal and non-verbal communication with your client (pacing). I created this rapport non-verbally with Fatima as she described her feelings of fear and anger about the war. Just listening and using reflective language in itself often allows a person's problem to be transformed.

Specify the Outcome

The most common way that new clients state their outcome is to say what they don't want (e.g., "I don't want my business to fail," "I don't want to feel anxious when I'm in a group"). Scott Miller and the other researchers in the solution focused therapy movement have shown that simply focusing people on what they want instead of what they don't enhances both commitment to coaching and success. (Miller et alia 1996). Guiding the person to do this involves using questions to help the person shift from general nominalizations ("I want happiness") and unspecified verbs ("I want to nurture myself more") to sensory specific descriptions ("I will take ten minutes each day to focus on what I have done well and write three examples of actions I'm pleased with in my diary"). Prior to the war, Fatima had been a medical student, and she wanted to recover from her panic so that she could be relaxed enough to successfully complete her studies.

Open Up the Client's Model of the World

Clients change when they believe they can change and that there is a reason to change. New clients frequently feel as if they are suffering as a result of events and responses they cannot control, and they hope that an NLP coach will magically "fix" their brain. My aim is instead to give them charge of their brain. I utilize their own motivation style (especially Towards–Away From) to create a compelling reason to change.

I also want to demonstrate that they can change. Scott Miller's collation of solution focused research suggests that all successful personal change is preceded by a change in the "locus of control" from external to internal (Miller et alia 1996). In their study of NLP psychotherapy, Martina Genser-

Medlitsch and Peter Schutz in Vienna also found this characteristic shift to clients experiencing themselves as in charge of their life ("at cause" in NLP terms). (Genser-Medlitsch, and Schütz, 1997)

I asked Fatima if she could get the feeling of panic just by thinking about the war. She could, and I pointed out "So that means that the feeling is a result of the way you think about that. You'd know if thinking about those experiences felt different in twenty minutes time wouldn't you?" Our question presupposed that her thinking strategies generate the problem and could be changed within twenty minutes in order to generate the solutions she wanted. In nodding her agreement, she accepted the reframing of her feelings as generated by her thinking, and accepted her changing quickly as a possibility.

Leading

Leading is the step in the RESOLVE model where the official "NLP change process" is done. One important aspect of selecting from the hundreds of NLP processes is to notice what "personal strengths" the client has and match these with NLP processes. Significantly, some clients describe their problem as an internal feeling response (demonstrating a "skill" with recreating a feeling from an earlier memory - what NLP calls anchoring) while some describe their problem in a more detached way (demonstrating a "skill" with what NLP calls dissociation). Some clients talk about their problem globally and some talk about their problem in intricate detail.

In the RESOLVE Model I recommend beginning with what clients are already good at, and then shifting to the opposite pole (what NLP calls "pacing and leading"). For example, Fatima was already good at anchoring herself into her memories of panic using sounds, so we had her remember the enjoyable sounds of a party in her pre-war life, and anchored that good feeling with a touch on her arm. This "resource anchor" created a safe state of mind for her to begin the simple NLP Trauma Recovery Process, in which we teach the person's brain to dissociate or step back from the traumatic memories. Dissociation is the opposite skill from anchoring.

Verify That Change Has Happened

A new, more positive response pattern can sometimes be "anchored" in place during the NLP session without the person's conscious mind realizing; just as at times a panic response happens when the person's conscious mind doesn't expect it. The conscious mind is the reality testing component of the brain, and after changing response patterns it is important for it to reality test and confirm the change.

Asking the person to notice and even celebrate the difference installs a solution focused pattern which allows change to continue. As mentioned, simply asking, "What has changed positively as a result of that last process?" increases reports of successful change from 33% to 60%. After doing the NLP trauma process, we had Fatima think of the most disturbing situations that she had experienced in the war. A little surprised, she smiled and said, "I'm seeing the pictures and it's as if they're just over there and I'm here." We test the change using the client's own convincer strategy.

Ecological Exit Process

Finally, it is important to have the client plan for the situations in which their new response will be useful and for situations which may challenge it or even temporarily evoke the old response. Prochaska and Diclemente say, "Just as one swallow doesn't make a spring, one slip doesn't make a fall." (Prochaska, Norcriss and Diclemente 1994 pp. 227)

Planning for such challenges also allows us to check if anything else needs to change to make the new response fit ecologically (in a way that works for the person's life as a whole system). This involves both future-pacing and tasking. With Fatima, we had her think into the future and notice that she could relax and still keep safe. When we met her again a year later she'd had no further panic attacks or nightmares, and was amazed to remember how disabling they had been. Her life was back on track.

Eye Movement Integration

The first technique for removing traumatic responses is a technique that involves the person trying to focus on a traumatic memory while moving their eyes rapidly from side to side and corner to corner.

Eye Movement Integration (EMI) was developed by NLP Trainers Connirae and Steve Andreas in 1989, based on their learning of "Editing" used by NLP co-developer John Grinder. Similar processes are noted in previous Reichian Therapy, and of course previously NLP trained psychologist Francine Shapiro developed a similar method called Eye Movement Desensitization and Reprocessing (EMDR).

Compared to EMDR, the original NLP process of EMI has less interest in creating a long therapeutic protocol, less interest in conscious memory restructuring, and more flexibility with the movements used. EMI also uses NLP insights about anchoring and eye movement accessing cues. Gestalt

Therapist Danie Beaulieu has built a more elaborate model around the method in her book Integral Eye Movement Therapy. Andrew Austin has a quicker protocol which he calls Integral Eye Movement Therapy (IEMT) on which the following notes are based.

For some time, it has been known that moving the eyes causes enormous floods of electrical information across the brain and for this reason, during brain scans, a person is usually instructed to hold their eyes still. We now have research showing that rapid side-to-side eye movements during an event or during active recall of an event prevent the recording of even short term memory traces, and that the result is not a re-ordering of those memories but an interference with the neural circuitry of the memory being formed or reconsolidated (see for example, Engelhard et alia, 2010). This is at least partially the effect of "The NLP Eye Movement process" taught by NP trainers Steve Andreas and Connirae Andreas, and of NLP trainer Andy Austin's "Integral Eye Movement Therapy". Separately from NLP, this kind of method is promoted as EMDR. By calling it "Editing" Grinder refers to it as a type of reconsolidation similar to that experienced by the mice in the experiment above, although instead of connecting the hippocampal memory to a positive place in the amygdala, it would then be connecting it to what Grinder calls a "Know Nothing State' (Grinder 2002)

While we do not have clinical research on this exact protocol for the Eye Movement process, we do have some dramatic research on EMDR, based on a very similar protocol. A 2012 study of 22 people found that EMDR therapy helped 77 percent of the individuals with psychotic disorder and PTSD. It found that their hallucinations, delusions, anxiety, and depression symptoms were significantly improved after treatment. The study also found that symptoms were not exacerbated during treatment. Only five of the twenty-two completers (22.7%) still met criteria for PTSD after treatment. (van den Berg and van der Gaag, 2012).

The elegance of the languaging added by Andy Austin is what makes his process truly efficient. Firstly, he has the person access the earliest memory that their brain can find where this specific emotion was activated. He does this by asking a series of questions which presuppose that a) the emotion must be strong to be a problem, b) if it is strong then it must be familiar and have happened many times, c) if it has happened many times, then there must be a much earlier time which they can remember, and d) since the feeling is so strong, the earlier memory must be quite vivid. This then allows a dramatic contrast when the person tries in vain to recall the same memory after the process. The process actually shifts the information in the brain so radically it is usually hard for the person to even recall what the emotion was like. If they still access a negative feeling when trying to think of the memory or original emotion, then the process is simply repeated *from the beginning* with this new emotion. The process is simply presented here for your information, and not to train you in its use. More thorough training in the process can be obtained via Andrew Austin.

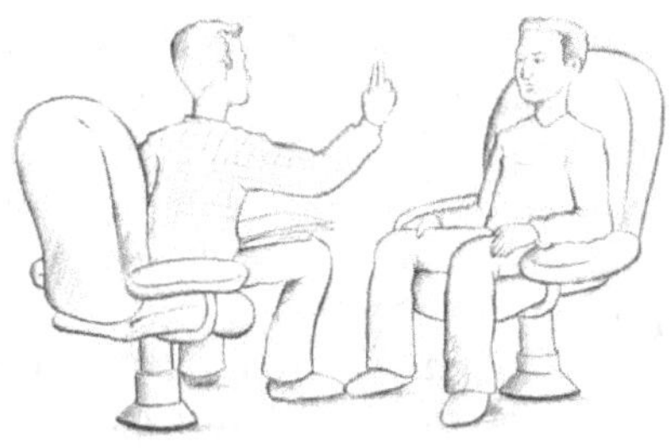

Eye Movement Integration
Adapted from Steve and Connirae Andreas and Danie Beaulieu
NB also Francine Shapiro and Andrew Austin

♦   Resourceful state for the Practitioner.

♦   Establish rapport

♦   Elicit the undesired state and scale using SUD (Subjective Units of Distress) 1-10 (Shapiro, 1995, p.62)

"Do what you usually do to create this feeling. What shall we call this feeling you want to change, and on a scale of 0-10, how strong is this feeling now, with 0 being nothing and 10 being as strong as it could be?"

*** "Find the earliest time you had this feeling at this intensity, and hold this memory in your mind as we do the process."**

Andrew Austin in Integral Eye Movement Therapy has 3 questions to elicit the earliest memory of the emotion, replacing this last question. Note this is not an EMDR or IEMT training. For more information on IEMT training see: Richards, 2021 p. 121-123
Ask: "And how familiar is *this* feeling"
Ask: "When was the first time that you can remember feeling this?"
Ask: "And how vivid is this memory now?"

♦   Do the Eye Movement Process (the primary 3 movements identified in EMDR, described below, are usually enough. See Shapiro, 1995, p64-65.)

"OK, look at the pen and hold your head still. As I move the pen, try to hold that memory and be aware of how you experience it."

Face the person with your hand holding the pen a meter from their face. Remind them to keep their head still. Use smooth even movements and a wide range. Move back and forward starting with horizontal movement and then move diagonally from corner to corner across the center. Do 5 movements each way. Ideally the client will report difficulty recalling the visual and auditory elements of the memory. Shapiro (1995, p. 64) suggests that circular movements can be used to calm down emotion also.

♦   Test and Futurepace
Test: "When you try access *that* feeling now how strong is it 0-10?"
Futurepace: "And when you think of a future time, when in the past *that* feeling might have come up, what happens now?"
If a negative kinesthetic emerges then repeat the process from the asterisked point above (*), locating the earliest memory again.

The NLP Trauma Recovery Process

This eye movement process above is one option for quickly eliminating traumatic responses. A second process is altering the perceptual position of consolidated long term memories towards what memory researchers refer to as observer memory (i.e. what NLP, with obstinacy, refers to as dissociation - Searching for Memory, Schachter, D.L., 1996, p 21-22). Observer memory is a type of reconsolidation that is done naturally in the brain over long periods of time, especially to distressing memories, and it also seems to require frontal cortex maturation (i.e. it cannot easily be done by a child of say 5 years old). In observer memory, the memory is recoded so that the person views it from outside as if watching it on a movie screen. The memory can thus be accessed without the amygdala being activated.

Research suggests that at times the original memory may be so altered by the eye movement processes, that it cannot be well retrieved. Clinically, we would be better doing eye movement processes with younger children, and with people very close in time to the events they are coping with. The possible loss of memory clarity would be a small price to pay for an effective protection from long term traumatisation. With longer term issues, the NLP Trauma recovery (Reconsolidation) process (also called the movie theatre technique) may give us better meaning elaboration and subsequent learning about the events being processed.

Training the brain to dissociate from disturbing events is a key to emotional health, as demonstrated in research by Brad Bushman and Dominik Mischkowski (2013). They subjected research students to a situation designed to evoke anger and anxiety. They then asked the students to review the events. Some students were told to adopt a self-immersed perspective ("see the situation unfold through your eyes as if it were happening to you all over again") and then analyze their feelings surrounding the event. Others were told to use the self-distancing perspective ("move away from the situation to a point where you can now watch the event unfold from a distance...watch the situation unfold as if it were happening to the distant you all over again") and then analyze their feelings. The third control group was not told how to view the scene or analyze their feelings. Each group was told the replay the scene in their minds for 45 seconds. The researchers then tested the participants for aggressive thoughts and angry feelings. The difference was dramatic; those students who had dissociated themselves were substantially less distressed and less angry.

This distancing is the basis of the famous NLP phobia-trauma process, from which the Memory Reconsolidation process is developed, which rehearses the brain to reconsolidate a memory as an observer experience by having the client visualise the event happening on a movie screen. In the process the movie is then re-run associated but in reverse, so that if the client ever accidentally steps back into the memory, it "auto-rewinds" like an old style VHS videotape which then pops out of the machine.

In his book "The Trauma Trap", Dr David Muss MD documents his extensive use of this NLP Trauma Process with victims of PTSD: A policeman involved in the Hillsborough soccer disaster describes how his flashbacks (sudden horrific memories of the trauma), insomnia and alcohol abuse disappeared after two sessions. A patient (Barbara Drake) tells how one session with Dr Muss completely resolved flashbacks and other symptoms resulting from a sexual abuse experience.

These and the other stories documented by Muss parallel our own experiences as trainers and Master Practitioners of NLP. Muss says "I know that it has worked for every patient I have dealt with so far, without exception." (Muss, "The Trauma Trap", 1991, p 10). Muss did a pilot study with 70 members of the West Midlands Police Force, who had witnessed major disasters such as the Lockerbie air crash. Of these, 19 qualified as having PTSD. The time between trauma and treatment varied from six weeks to ten years. All participants reported that after an average of three sessions they were completely free of intrusive memories and other PTSD symptoms. Follow-up ranged from 3 months to 2 years, and all gains were sustained over that time.

Testing it in Sarajevo

In 1993, I was invited to Sarajevo, in war-torn Bosnia-Herzegovina, to run a two day training course. We taught a group of thirty people, most of whom were Psychiatrists, some of whom were Charge Nurses or Social Workers. The course was run at the Kosevo Clinic, Sarajevo's central Psychiatric Hospital. Our course materials were translated by a number of people in New Zealand and in Sarajevo, and one of the hospital's Computer Centre organisers, Dubravko Vanicek, was our interpreter at the training. After only two days training, over three quarters of those professionals who trained with us in Sarajevo said they now planned to use the methods we taught.

For example, Dr Cerny Kulenovic described the model as "Definitely useful. We used it on ourselves and we treated our colleagues too. We got the predicted effects…. We were well informed and gained very good results in the second day. A new treatment which was economical, short and successful." Dr Mehmedika Suljic Enka agreed "This training gives more practice in dealing with survivors of traumatic experiences or clients with phobias. Used with my own similar problem, it helped to relieve my fear, and I realised how I can help other people. I have improved my knowledge in Psychiatry." For me, the ease with which the process worked in this most extreme of situations was so inspiring it began a whole new phase of my career, culminating in this book!

Testing it in the USA

In 2001, after the 9/11 attacks, New York NLP organisations offered free dissociation trauma cure treatments for New York citizens. their results, over hundreds of people, were so promising that they gained the attention of authorities. In 2014, NLP Trainers, Dr Frank Bourke, Dr Richard Gray and colleagues received a $300,000 grant from New York state and over 50 War Veterans Organisations referred clients to begin a pilot study on their development of the method, called RTM or Reconsolidation of Traumatic Memories. 58 veterans were interviewed and evaluated for treatment (52 diagnosed with PTSD). Nearly all of them were combat vets, and they ranged from Vietnam veterans suffering for almost 50 years to vets from Iraq and Afghanistan. Of 33 clients who entered treatment, 26 (using the national PTSD norm of 45 points as cutoff) no longer test as having PTSD; their symptoms were fully alleviated in under five sessions. There were six others who either dropped out or had missing diagnostic scores; one more did not respond to the treatment.

As the protocol was tested under strict scientific standards for the first time, it produced results that matched previous success levels. In this study 75% of the treatment pool and 96% of program completers terminated treatment with complete and permanent elimination of the symptoms of PTSD in less than 5 hours of treatment as verified at the two- and six-week follow-ups. The researchers say "According to combined behavioral and instrumental measures, this pilot completely removed the PTSD diagnosis in 96% of those who completed treatment. Current VA and Army treatments "statistically improve" PTSD scores 35% of the time (Steenkamp & Litz (2013, 2014). No currently approved treatments for PTSD remove the diagnosis; at best, they only improve the symptom scores." See Gray and Liotta (2012) for historical details.

The validation of this initial research in subsequent studies has been NLP's most successful research project to date. The NLP Fast Rewind Movie process ("Phobia cure") was redesigned and repurposed as The Reconsolidation of Traumatic Memories (RTM) process. Using the PCL-5 checklist (appendixed below), research results were dramatic.

- Pilot Study: Journal of Military, Veteran, and Family Health. 25 of 26 (96%) no longer test as having PTSD. (Gray and Bourke, 2015)
- First Replication Study. 28 of 30 (94%) no longer test as having PTSD. (Tylee, Gray et alia, 2016)
- Second Replication Study (women). 29 of 30 (96%) no longer test as having PTSD. (Tylee, Gray et alia, 2016)
- Third Replication Study. 68 of 75 (90%) no longer test as having PTSD. (Steenkamp, Litz et alia, 2016)

The following instructions for the process are detailed, so that even a person who has not trained in NLP could utilise them. While this is not my recommendation, I realise that if I publish this book with less detailed instructions, the risk of misuse may be increased. The detailed instructions here have indeed been used in Trauma recovery centres by people not trained in NLP, but there the users are working with a background of experience in PTSD.

Preparing for the NLP Trauma Recovery Process

1. Be in a Resourceful State Yourself, and Establish Rapport

As a person guiding someone through this process, you may be about to hear some disturbing stories that you want to stay dissociated from. You may be about to see people in profound distress. It may be useful to stack a few more resources on to your own resource anchor (see the chapter on anchoring), and create a 'thought' access for it (not only pressing fingers together or similar) like a 'word' or a colour or phrase, so you can quickly regain resourceful state each time.

Be aware of your response to others: especially if you are working in larger centres where there will be an sense of connectedness. This could mean that emotional events (e.g. more bad news, somebody turning up with anger...) can shift the whole room full of people (they may have all been in rapport for a few days). Become aware of the 'rapport leader' and get in rapport with them, if ecological and ethical, so you can reframe carefully.
Match the person's breathing, posture and voice, and reflective listen.

2. Check Their Resourcefulness and Create Rapport

Is the person able to stay calm enough to talk to you about something pleasant or neutral? If not (i.e. you calibrate the person is distressed or they tell you they are distressed) check with them whether they want to learn how to relax now, so that the experience is easier (this is useful as they may have some misconceptions about an NLP session being the same as a counselling session - i.e. that you need to talk about painful experiences, this would be an opportunity to teach them it will be different to that). If, after helping/teaching them how to relax, this is still difficult you may need to arrange to conduct the session at a later time.

There may be some obvious acute physical responses to anxiety that you need to be prepared for; vomiting, hyperventilation, fainting or screaming. We would suggest you have a "first aid kit" handy for such times, which could include a discretely placed bucket, tissues, and a soft cushion / place to lie down.

Stay in rapport without getting caught up in their emotions.
- Breathe in time with the person
- Sit in a similar position to them
- Use similar voice tone, speed and volume
- Restate their comments to confirm you've understood

3. Check What Problems the Person Has Been Experiencing

What symptoms of trauma does the person experience? Briefly ask them to tell you, and reflective listen (restate what they say). Reassure them this can change. The Posttraumatic Stress Disorder (PTSD) Checklist (PCL-5) can be given to the person before the following process and then again perhaps 3 weeks after, to provide more reliable evidence of change. Post Traumatic Stress Disorder (DSM-IV 309.81) symptoms include:

- repeated, distressing memories / dreams of event
- acting or feeling as if the event were still happening
- intense distress when exposed to images or sounds resembling the event
- efforts to avoid anything that could remind the person of the event
- inability to experience a normal range of emotions and interest in life
- not planning as if life had a future
- difficulty concentrating, or relaxing, or difficulty sleeping
- sudden anger / Startle responses
- nightmares or sleep disturbances

Are there any other problems you need to know about (for example, medical problems)?

The scaling question could be asked before beginning the script. It says: "On a scale of 1 (neutral or calm) to 10 (the worst they can think of) how bad does it feel now?" You can use this same question in follow-up to check the success of the process.

4. Set the Goal

How would the person be acting, thinking and feeling if these problems were solved? If this person's problems were solved, what else would change? Is that okay for them? If not, ask what they need to do to make it okay for them. You are checking for ecology issues e.g. that the person is afraid that if they don't have their panic, they might not keep themselves/others safe. If there are such objections, they can be reframed by a statement like this:

"Now I know that there's a part of you that thought it was important for you to hold on to those old feelings. A part of you may have been trying to keep you safe, or to make sure that you really learned the lesson of this event. But holding on to the feeling hasn't actually kept you safe. It has made your life more dangerous by having you live in fear. If that part of you really wants you to have learned from that event, then it will really keep you safe by letting go of the feeling now, and keeping the things you needed to learn."

5. Give an Overview of the Process

E.g. "This whole process usually takes less than half an hour. The aim is for you to feel relatively comfortable throughout. Most people find that their symptoms disappear immediately. Your brain learns new responses very quickly." You may give The Person An Experience Of How The Way They Imagine Things Causes Their Body To Respond eg Have the person turn around with their arm stretched out pointing. Tell them "Just go round carefully to where your arm feels tight, and see where you're pointing.... Now come back to the front.... Now imagine turning round again, but this time imagine that your body flows easily way round further, perhaps twenty or thirty centimetres further than before. You'd be pointing at a totally different place. What would you be saying to yourself if you went around that far?... and now turn around with that same hand and see how far you go NOW!"

Use Language That Creates Positive Internal Representations of Success. Rather than "This may be scary", say "I'm not saying this will be totally comfortable". Once you've started, refer to "the way you used to feel when you thought of this" and "the problem you had", placing the difficulty in the past.

6. Explain Dissociation in NLP Terms

E.g. "We are going to teach your brain to react differently to the memories of the event. People can remember events in two different ways. If you think of a simple, enjoyable event you've experienced recently, like eating breakfast today [choose another event if breakfast reminds the person of the trauma], you can remember what you saw through your own eyes [wait for the person to remember] and enjoy all the feelings of eating that breakfast. It may even make your mouth water. That's one way to remember it. Another way to remember it is to imagine seeing yourself sitting in the room eating. Watch yourself over there eating, as if you were watching from a distance. Even make a still picture of yourself, like a photograph, perhaps a black and white photograph. When you see that picture, it's not so easy to get the feeling of enjoying eating breakfast. You need to step back into your body to taste it again. It's quite okay to remember the feeling in your body eating breakfast. But there are some things it's better to step back from, so you can see what happens, but you feel separate from it. People who are enjoying their life can choose which way to remember each thing. We are going to teach your brain to automatically remember those old unpleasant events in a way that keeps you separate from the feelings you had then. That means the other problems you've had will disappear, and you'll get the enjoyment you want in life. Does that sound useful?"

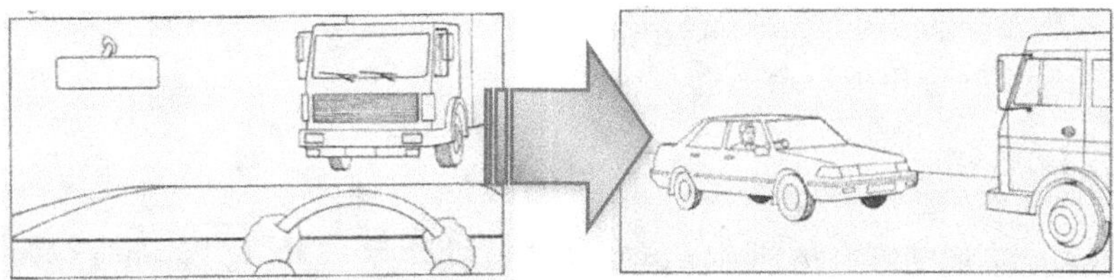

Following is a very detailed and slightly elaborated version of the process used in the research above. It is written in such detail so that even people new to the process can benefit, and was checked with one of the developers of RTM, Steve Andreas.

A Sample Script For The NLP Trauma Recovery Process Itself

1.   Establish Rapport, Set Up Resource Anchor

"Before we start, what I'd like you to do is to remember a time when you felt in charge of what you were doing, perhaps when you were doing something you know how to do [like baking a cake, or driving a car], and get back the memory of a specific time, so you can step into your body at that time, and see what you saw, hear the sounds, and fell the feeling of being in charge. Now, as you feel that feeling, I want you to press together the thumb and little finger of your left hand and enjoy the sense of being in charge ... Great; now release the fingers and come back to being in the room here, and stretch."

Repeat for two other positive feelings instead of "being in charge" e.g. "confidence", relaxation", "humour". Your being able to create that positive feeling in yourself as they think of it will also help. If they can't think of a time when they felt positive, have them remember a time when someone they like had that feeling, and feel what that person must have felt like.

2.   Test Resource Anchor

"OK, now stretch and have a look out the window. Just see something you didn't notice before ... Good; now press that thumb and little finger together and feel the difference."

Check that the anchor (thumb-finger touch) causes the person to shift their breathing/body position/facial expression back to a positive state similar to the one they used remembering the times. If not, repeat step one, emphasising their re-experiencing each positive state.

3.   Pretest

"Right, now before we start, I just want to check this thing that has been a problem. I'd like you to just briefly think about the things that have been upsetting you. What does it feel like to remember that? On a scale of 1 to 10 where 1 is calm and neutral and 10 is the worst imaginable, how does it feel now?"

Check for a clear shift in breathing, body posture and facial expression. If you need to, to draw them back out, have them stand up and press the thumb and little finger together until they are out of the memory.

"OK. Come back to here now. You'll know when that changes now won't you?"

4.   Set Up The Movie Theatre

"Now panic attacks [*or* "flashbacks/nightmares/Post Traumatic Stress/phobias like you've been having"] is just a result of the brain having a scary experience and storing it in a less than useful way. The brain did that the first time you had that experience, and it took it less than 30 seconds to do. So its just that easy to change once we know how the brain did that."

"To change it, what we need to do first is set up a kind of movie theatre here. You've been to a movie sometime, so you know there are seats here [*point to movie theatre seat*] and a screen up here [*point to front -ideally a blank wall*]. And sitting in the movie theatre here, I want you to see a picture up on the screen, of yourself, a black and white photo. It could be of the way you look now, or of you doing something you do at home, or just a photo like a recent one you've seen in a photo album ... Have you done that?"

"Good. Now, before you had that experience that was scary, there was a time when it hadn't happened yet, and you were safe. Take all the time you need to remember that time, and make a picture of yourself at that safe time before the event. Put that picture of you looking safe before the event up on the screen now, and turn it to black and white too. Have you done that?"

"Great. And after that experience that was scary, there was a time when it was over, and although you still had memories of the event, you were physically safe. Take time to remember that safe time after it happened, and put a picture of yourself at that time on the screen. Have you done that too?"

n.b. if there has not yet been a time that is physically safe, you may need to create an imaginary time in the future.

"OK. Now I'd like you to stand up out of that chair and come back here. This is a chair in the projection room from where they show the movie [*seat the person now in the second chair, behind the movie theatre chair*]. There's a glass screen through which you can see the movie theatre and you can see that other you sitting in the movie theatre, watching a black and white photo on the screen. Can you see that person in the theatre seat?"

Always speak to the person as if they are actually in the theatre when they sit on the theatre seat. Always speak as if they are actually in the projection booth when they sit in the projection booth seat. If, while in the projection booth seat, the person begins to talk about what it was like inside the traumatic experience, have them stand up and move "out of the projection booth". You want both seats safely separated from the memory.

If the person starts to re-associate into the memory and panic, your choices include:
> a)   *Have the person stand up and fire their resource anchor.*
> b)   *Walk around the room with them.*
> c)   *Have the person get out of the projection booth and imagine they are further away from the movie screen.*

5.   Run The Movie Forward "Dissociated"

"So now, as you stay in the projection room, safe behind the glass, you can run the movies, and watch as that other person in the theatre watches them. And because there are holes on the side of the glass, you can hear the movie, because we're going to show a movie soon. And you'll be safe and comfortable here, maybe with something nice to eat and drink while you watch the person watching the movie."

"What I want you to do is to run a movie of yourself in that time when the unpleasant event happened. The movie will start before the event, at the time when you were safe before, and will run through the time after the event, once you were physically safe again. Like any movie, it will show the important parts of the story, form beginning to end, but this movie will be in black and white, like an old film.

OK? Now, while you run the movie, I'd like you to watch that person the movie theatre. They may have some response to the movie, but you're in the projection room, so just run it through and watch their watching. OK, go ahead, and tell me when you're done."

6.   Fast Rewind the Movie "Associated"

"Now, in a moment, I'm going to get you to pretend that you float out of the projection room and into the movie at that safe end scene. It may help you to close your eyes to imagine that. Once you're in the movie, in the body of that earlier you, turn the movie to colour. Then we're going to run the movie backwards, from the end to that safe beginning, but fast, like fast rewind on a video. You've seen a video rewind, but this will go so fast the whole thing will only take a second and a half, so it goes zziiiiiiipp! Got that? Okay, now; float into the movie, at the end, turn it colour and zziiiiiipp! ... Once you're done, turn the movie back to black and white, and float back to where you actually are, here in the projection room ... Hi."

7.   Repeat until Change Occurs

"OK. Now I want you to be here in the projection booth and watch again as that person in the movie theatre sees the movie through from safe beginning to safe end ... OK? Great; and again, imagine you float into the end and turn the movie to colour, then run it backwards zziiiiiipp, and come back to the projection booth once its done ..."

"Great. Have a stretch ... Now try and get back that picture at the start of the movie [*If they can't, go to step 8*]. Now again, watch from the movie projection booth as that person watches the black and white movie, float into the safe end and run it backwards fast in colour, and come back here. Tell me when you're done...".

"Good. Now I want you to try to do this process, a bit faster, and do it through as many times as it takes till you can't get back the movie, or you realise that the feeling has suddenly gone. Some people say the movie gets blank spots and fades out; some say it's as if the tape snaps. It's probably started already. Just go ahead and try to run the movie each way till you know you can't. Then tell me ...".

8.   Verify Change (Post-test)

"Great. ,And notice that the feeling went with the picture. Okay; now stretch and look out the window. Notice something there you haven't seen before ...".

"Okay, now what I want you to do is have a go at remembering that time, and try and get back the feelings you used to have about it." [*Smile*]. "How's that now? Different!"

Check from the person's body posture, breathing and facial expression that this is a different, more relaxed response than the pretest.

"Now I'm not suggesting you'll enjoy that thing now. Just that the uncomfortable feeling is gone. There's often a little uncertainty, as you try to go to remember, because this was a reliable response you had. You had that problem for a while, and it's strange for it to be different, now. Pretty amazing isn't it?" [*Try again until the person realises it's different*].

9.   Ecology Check and Future Pace

"Now one thing that has happened occasionally, is that when someone had an anxiety, it gave them something to do. So now it's important to find out what you can do instead. I'd like you to think of a future time, the kind of time when, in the past, you would have responded in that old way; and notice what you're doing instead, and how you're feeling. How is that? ...".

"And think of another situation when, in the past, you'd have had that problem. How is it different now? ... Is that okay for all of you?"

"On a scale of 1 (neutral or calm) to 10 (the worst you can think of) how does it feel *now*?"

"Excellent. Welcome to your new life. That was big change wasn't it!"

Appendix:
The Posttraumatic Stress Disorder (PTSD) Checklist (PCL-5)

The Posttraumatic Stress Disorder (PTSD) Checklist is known as the PCL, it is a self-screening tool to help in the diagnosis of PTSD. Even lay persons can safely use this questionnaire, following the included instructions. They may then be able to contribute to the growing research validating the techniques you have read about above.

The PCL only gives a probable diagnosis of PTSD; a definitive diagnosis can only be given by an appropriately qualified clinician. The Posttraumatic Stress Disorder Checklist has four different versions, the version which is most suitable in your case depends on either the psychiatric manual being used for the clinician, or the type of stressful experience that has/may have caused the problems you experience. The different PCL versions are: PCL-5 for PTSD diagnosis using the new DSM-5 psychiatric manual (released 2013) PCL-C for Civilians, for diagnosis using the DSM-IV psychiatric manual PCL-M for Military veterans or service personnel, for diagnosis using the DSM-IV psychiatric manual PCL-S for non-military use, based on a Specific very stressful event rather than multiple events, for diagnosis using the DSM-IV psychiatric manual.

PCL-5: Posttraumatic Checklist for DSM-5 Instructions: There is one question about the stressful experience or event, followed by 20 multiple-choice questions below. These questions have been designed for adults. If you prefer you can download a printable version of this screening tool instead. The questions below are from the PCL-5, which applies to all types of stressful experiences. Disclaimer This self-assessment tool is not a substitute for clinical diagnosis or advice. By using the tool you agree to accept that the distributors and contributors are not responsible or liable for the outcome of the tool, the accuracy of the calculations, or any decisions or events which result from using it. This source does not provide medical advice.

"What is the specific, worst stressful experience you remember?" The helper writes a description of this: This can later be used by a clinician and compared against the types of "qualifying event" that are known to be possible causes of PTSD.

"A person who has had an extremely stressful experience may have many a range of different problems as a result of the stressful experience. Some people have had more than one extremely stressful experience. For each of the questions below, keep your worst experience or event in mind, please read each problem carefully and then select one response to indicate how much you have been bothered by that problem in the past month."

Rate each as:
Not at all –0
A little bit –1
Moderately –2
Quite a bit –3
Extremely – 4

In the past month, how much were you bothered by:
1. Repeated, disturbing, and unwanted memories of the stressful experience?
2. Repeated, disturbing dreams of the stressful experience?
3. Suddenly feeling or acting as if the stressful experience were actually happening again (as if you were actually back there reliving it)?
4. Feeling very upset when something reminded you of the stressful experience?

5. Having strong physical reactions when something reminded you of the stressful experience (for example, heart pounding, trouble breathing, sweating)?

6. Avoiding memories, thoughts, or feelings related to the stressful experience?

7. Avoiding external reminders of the stressful experience (for example, people, places, conversations, activities, objects, or situations)?

8. Trouble remembering important parts of the stressful experience?

9. Having strong negative beliefs about yourself, other people, or the world (for example, having thoughts such as: I am bad, there is something seriously wrong with me, no one can be trusted, the world is completely dangerous)?

10. Blaming yourself or someone else for the stressful experience or what happened after it?

11. Having strong negative feelings such as fear, horror, anger, guilt, or shame?

12. Loss of interest in activities that you used to enjoy?

13. Feeling distant or cut off from other people?

14. Trouble experiencing positive feelings (for example, being unable to feel happiness or have loving feelings for people close to you)?

15. Irritable behavior, angry outbursts, or acting aggressively?

16. Taking too many risks or doing things that could cause you harm?

17. Being "superalert" or watchful or on guard?

18. Feeling jumpy, or easily startled?

19. Having difficulty concentrating?

20. Trouble falling or staying asleep?

PCL-5, © Weathers, F. W., Litz, B. T., Keane, T. M., Palmieri, P. A., Marx, B. P., & Schnurr, P. P. (2013). Scoring The score is worked out by adding up the number of points for each answer. The minimum score is 0, the maximum is 80.

Try it yourself online: http://traumadissociation.com/pcl5-ptsd

Result Explained: There are several different ways of interpreting the scores given by the PTSD Checklist-5. For a person to have a probable diagnosis of PTSD sufficient criteria must be at least moderately met in each of the four symptom groups. This means you need to have one or more symptoms from questions 1 to 5, either question 6 or 7, two or more from questions 8 to 14, and two or more from questions 15 to 20, each of which must be met moderately, quite a bit or extremely. In addition, a score of 38 or higher indicates probable PTSD in veterans; the score may be set higher or lower for civilians; no agreement has been reached yet since it was only developed after the DSM-5 was published in 2013. A lower cut off may be used for initial screening rather than probable diagnosis, the maximum score is 80. For those people already diagnosed, it can be used to measure improvement. A definite diagnosis can only be given by a clinician, and depends on the details of the extremely stressful experience described at the top of the form and the effect on the individual, a clinician would also need to ask questions about the problems to check the person's understanding of each question and that the PTSD criteria are fully met. The PCL-5 scores are not comparable with scores from the PCL-C, PCL-M or PCL-S because the number of questions and points per question differ.

Measuring improvements in PTSD: The PCL5-PTSD tool can be used multiple times after diagnosis to assess the change in PTSD symptoms over time. A reduction of 5 points has been suggested to reflect a reliable reduction in symptoms, meaning the change is not caused by chance. This can be used to check if an individual's symptoms are responding to treatment. A 10-20 point reduction reflects clinically significant change.

Key Concept: NLP Trauma Recovery Process

This process teaches the brain how to "dissociate" (use observer memory), and now has a long history of excellent controlled research esp. in USA
1. As a guide, be in a resourceful state, Create rapport.
2. Set a relaxation anchor (see in earlier chapter)
3. Pretest "You'd know if that changed, wouldn't you?"
4. Explain the process. Set up movie theatre, choose before & after scenes.
5. Go back to the projection booth seat. Run a movie dissociated from safe before to safe after, in black & white. Watch yourself in the theatre as that you is watching the movie.
6. Step into the movie at safe end, turn it to colour, and run it back to the safe start, using ultra-fast rewind with you inside it.
7. Repeat until the person reports a visual or kinesthetic change.
8. Verify the change. Think of a past time when this was an issue and notice that now it feels different.
9. Think of a future time when that would have previously been a problem. Check the change feels good.

Key Concept: NLP Eye Movement Process with Andy Austin's IEMT Language Model

This process recreates the memory reconsolidation state that occurs in REM sleep. Research on the similar but more elaborated EMDR system shows it is highly successful.

The process has 3 sections:
1) Assess the emotional state using 1-10 scaling and the familiarity of it at this level. Elicit first memory of the traumatic response and check that it feels strong.
2) Have the person try to hold onto that memory while they keep their head very still and move their eyes side to side and corner to opposite corner about 4 times each direction.
3) Test the memory, and then the emotional response, and then the imagined response to future events.

Practical Exercise Day 10: Eye Movement Process Based on IEMT

Select an experience of your own that is unpleasant enough so you want to change it, but comfortable enough so you can still follow instructions.

a) Begin by being confident that this is a natural process you are re-activating.
b) Step into the undesired emotional state. Out of ten, how strong is *this* feeling, with ten being as strong as it can be?"
c) And how familiar is *this* feeling?
d) And when was the first time that I can remember feeling *this* feeling… now … it may not be the first time it ever happened, but rather the first time that I can remember now?
e) And notice how vivid is this memory now?
f) Do the Eye Movement Process. As you move your eyes from corner to corner and side to side, hold that memory vividly in your mind for as long as possible… and if that memory fades, try very hard to bring it back… try as hard as you can to retain that experience."
g) Perform The Three tests
Test 1. Ask: "And how does *that* memory feel now?"
Test 2. Ask: "And what happens when I try access *that* feeling now?"
Test 3. Ask: "And when I think about the possibility of *that* kind of event in the future now, what comes up for me now?"
h) If it still doesn't feel comfortable, then repeat the process and locate next memory. Do not just go back to moving the eyes! Go back to c) above, assuming the feeling is in some way a "different" feeling, possibly with a different level from 0-10.

Chapter 11:
Skills for The End of the World?

If there was one book you could take with you to a world where civilization and the ecosystem are both in collapse, what would it be? Chris Begley is an archaeologist and wilderness survival instructor. He is a professor of anthropology at Transylvania University. He is often asked what skills we need most of all to face a future where civilization itself is collapsing.

He says "While the wilderness survival skills certainly can't hurt, it will be empathy, generosity, and courage that we need to survive. Kindness and fairness will be more valuable than any survival skill. Then as now, social and leadership skills will be valued. We will have to work together. We will have to grow food, educate ourselves, and give people a reason to persevere. The needs will be enormous, and we cannot run away from that. Humans evolved attributes such as generosity, altruism, and cooperation because we need them to survive. Armed with those skills, we will turn towards the problem, not away from it. We will face the need, and we will have to solve it together. That is the only option. That's what survival looks like."

That is what you have been learning in this book. Finally, what you have been learning are the skills that have enabled our ancestors to survive through millions of challenging years on this planet, to grow through the rise and fall of thousands of cultures. These same skills will enable us to survive far into the future and reach out to the stars themselves, which in a sense gave us birth.

Aligning Neurological Levels

One of the characteristics of resilience noted by the American Psychological Association is the ability to step back and see the bigger picture in life, in this way. NLP Trainer Robert Dilts has developed a model for thinking about the "level" at which a person is making changes in their life, which gives us a concrete way to do just that. He calls it the Neurological Levels Model (Dilts, 1996, p 18-23). Put simply, whenever a person has a problem they'd like to change, they're in a sense saying "I can't do that here." about their goal.

The most superficial level of working with this statement is to change the environment (the word "here") e.g. "If you can't do it here, why not move to another town, or get another job, or find a new relationship...."

The next level is to change the "that" -the specific behaviour that was the problem. This is the level that behaviour therapy works at. In NLP terms, this might mean using anchoring to anchor in a new response to that particular situation, or it might mean doing the NLP Memory Reconsolidation Process on it.

At a deeper level you could change the person's capabilities, the "do" part of the sentence. By teaching the person a new strategy such as a relaxation process, or the Key Questions Process, you could enable them to respond to a whole range of situations more resourcefully and capably.

At an even deeper level, though, even capabilities are a result of the person's beliefs about what is possible. At the level of beliefs (the word "can't") we could use deeper NLP processes to remove the limiting belief. This would enable the person to generate whole new strategies. Even deeper than this, a person's beliefs are a result of their sense of identity (the word "I"). A person who experiences themselves as a failure develops beliefs to support that self-image and strategies to prove those beliefs are true. Some NLP processes also work at the identity level to change the person's whole experience of what is them and what is not them.

And there's one deeper level to work at; the moment before the person says anything. That's what you could call the spiritual level, the level at which they have a sense of life and the universe as much larger than they themselves are. This process is designed to work at this much deeper level.

Aligning Neurological Levels
From Robert Dilts

1. Choose a problem you've had, and would like to change in a fundamental way.

2. Stand somewhere with plenty of space in front of you (enough to step forward six times). Think of the environment where the problem occurs. Notice what you see, and listen to the sounds there.

3. Take a step forward. Consider what you actually do and say in the problem situation. Just run a movie of what happens. It is important not to criticise yourself for what you do, and not to justify yourself. Simply notice what happens.

4. Take another step forward. When you do those things, what capabilities, what skills are you using? And what skills are you not using? In a way the

things you do come in a pattern, a habitual response – that is what we mean by a "skill".

5. Take another step forward. Consider what beliefs you are acting on in that situation. What feels important to you in that situation? (not what you think should be important now; what really feels important when you are there? – it may be just getting out of the situation) What do you find yourself believing about your potential, about others who are there, and about the situation?

6. Take another step forward. Who are "you" in this situation? What kind of person are you in this situation? If we only ever met you in this situation, who would we be meeting?

7. Take another step forward, and remember that you are here for a reason. You only got yourself into that situation because, in a wider sense, you're here on earth for a reason. Maybe you were trying to do something and got into this situation by accident, or maybe you chose to be in this situation, and then discovered it had challenges. But in either case this situation connects you to the bigger story of your life. You may not know in words what your reason is, but notice it now. Realise that this "reason" connects you to something vast. It connects you to the story of your family, your community, of the planet…. And even more. You may think of the big story it connects you to, as the history of humanity, as the laws of physics, as God, the Goddess, the universe, beingness, or just humanity. But it is a vast source of energy, in front of you now.

8. Take another step forward, into that source of energy. Feel its power. The energy that brings the stars into being.

9. As you feel that power, take a step back and notice how that power gives renewed strength to your mission, your reason. Take another step back and feel how that power transforms your sense of who you are (even in that situation you were thinking of). Take another step back and feel how that power therefore changes what you believe about that situation you were considering; and changes what seems important there. Some things that felt important don't even matter, and some things that you weren't even noticing may be the most important things happening. Take another step back and notice how it changes what skills you can use there. Remember now that you have so many skills to choose from, from your own story and from the greater story you are part of. Take another step back and be aware of how using those skills, with that vast power, changes what you will do and say there… changes every moment, every thought, every movement. Take

another step back and be aware how those actions, done with that power, will change the situation itself.

10. Thank that power.

Key Concept: Neurological Levels

The Neurological Levels model was developed by NLP Trainer Robert Dilts. There are 6 levels that any challenge can be viewed on and 6 levels that change can be made.
1) Environment
2) Behaviour
3) Capabilities
4) Beliefs and Values
5) Identity
6) Spirituality

Practical Exercise Day 11: Neurological Levels Alignment

Use this YouTube video to guide yourself through the process.
https://www.youtube.com/watch?v=Xu0Yfy53iXw

Bibliography:

International Coaching Federation (2012), 2012 Global Coaching Survey, 2012

Acosta, J. and Prager, J. (2002) *The Worst is Over* Jodere Publishing Group, San Diego

Andreas, C. (1992) *Successful Parenting: An Audio Cassette Program* NLP Comprehensive, Boulder, Colorado

Andreas, S. (2010) *Help With Negative Self Talk* Real People Press, Moab, Utah

Andreas, S. (1991) *Virginia Satir: The Patterns of her Magic* Science and Behaviour Books, Palo Alto, California, 1991

Andreas, S., (2012) *Transforming Negative Self-Talk: Practical, Effective Exercises*, W. W. Norton & Company, New York

Armstrong, T. (1993) *7 Kinds Of Smart*, Plume/Penguin, New York, 1993

Armstrong, T. (1997) *The Myth of the ADD Child* Penguin, Harmondsworth, England, 1997

Austin, Andrew, (2010) Integral Eye Movement Therapy Practitioner DVD Set, IEMT, London

Baldwin, A., Kalhoun, J., and Breese, F., (1945) "Patterns of Parent Behaviour" in *Psychological Monographs*, 1945, 58 (3)

Bandler, R. (1985) *Using Your Brain For A Change*, Real People Press, Moab, Utah

Bandler, R. and Grinder, J. (1979) *Frogs Into Princes* Real People Press, Moab, Utah

Bandler, R. and Grinder, J. (1975) *The Structure of Magic*. Cupertino, California: Meta Publications

Bandler, R. and Grinder, J. (1975), *Patterns of the Hypnotic Techniques of Milton H. Erickson, M.D. Volume 1*, Meta, Cupertino, California

Bandler, R. and La Valle, J. (1996) *Persuasion Engineering*™ Meta Publications, Capitola, California

Bandler, R., Grinder, J. and Satir, V. (1976) *Changing With Families*, Science and Behaviour Books, Palo Alto, California

Barkley, R. (1990) *Attention Deficit Hyperactivity Disorder: A handbook For Diagnosis and Treatment* Guilford, New York

Beaulieu, Danie, (2004) *Eye Movement Integration Therapy*, Crown Publishing, Bancyfelin, Wales

Begley, C. (2019) "I study collapsed civilizations. Here's my advice for a climate change apocalypse." Access on line 24/09/2019 at: https://www.kentucky.com/opinion/op-ed/article235384162.html

Blackerby, D.A. (1996) *Rediscover The Joy Of Learning*, Success Skills, Oklahoma

Bolstad, R. (2002) *RESOLVE: A New Model of Therapy*. Carmarthen, Wales, Crown Publishing

Bolstad, R. (2002) *Transforming Communication_* Pearsons, Auckland

Bolstad, R. (2010) "The How Behind The Secret" *Acuity the ANLP Journal*, Issue 1

Bolstad, R. and Hamblett, M. "Preventing Violence In Schools: An NLP Solution" p 3-14 in *Anchor Point*, Vol 14, No. 9, September 2000

Bonanno, G.E. (2004) "Loss. Trauma and Human Resilience" American Psychologist, January 2004, Vol. 59, No. 1

Booth, P. (1992) *Edmund Hillary: The Life of a Legend*, Moa Beckett, Auckland, 1992

Bushman, G. Kross, E. and Mischkowski, D. (2013) *Journal of Experimental Social Psychology*

Butcher, M. (2001) "Is Steve Gurney Mad" p 48-59 in *North & South*, July 2001

Byrne, R. (2006) *The Secret.* New York: Atria Books,

Canfield, J. and Hansen, M.V. (1993) *A 2nd Helping of Chicken Soup For The Soul.* Deerfield Beach, Florida: Health Communications Inc

Carkhuff, R.R. and Berenson, B.G. (1997) *Beyond Counselling and Therapy*, New York: Holt, Rinehart and Winston

Cedar, R. (1985) *A Meta-analysis of the Parent Effectiveness Training Outcome Research Literature*, Ed D. Dissertations, Boston University

Charvet, S.R. (2006) *Words That Change Minds*, Kendall/Hunt, Dubuque, Iowa,

Coddington, D. (2000) "Disciplined to Death" p 32-44 in *North & South*, February 2000

Condon, W. and Sander, L. (1974) "Neonate Movement Is Synchronised With Adult Speech: Interactional Participation and Language Acquisition" in *Science*, January 1974

Condon, W. S. (1982) "Cultural Microrhythms" p 53-76 in Davis, M. (ed) *Interactional Rhythms: Periodicity in Communicative Behaviour* Human Sciences Press, New York

Coyle, J.T. (2000) "Psychotropic Drug Use in Very Young Children" Editorial in *Journal of the American Medical Association*, Vol 283, No. 8, February 23, 2000

Craldell, J.S. (1989) "Brief treatment for adult children of alcoholics: Accessing resources for self care"p 510-513 in *Psychotherapy*, Volume 26, No 4, Winter, 1989

Crum, A.J. and Langer, E.J., (2007) "Mind-Set Matters: Exercise and the Placebo Effect" p 165-171 in *Psychological Science*, Volume 18, Issue 2, February 2007

Davison, G.C., and Neale, J.M., (1986) *Abnormal Psychology*, John Wiley & Sons, New York, 1986

De Bono, E. (1995) *Surpetition* Harper Collins, London

DeLozier, J. and Grinder, J. (1987) *Turtles All The Way Down* Grinder, DeLozier and Associates, Bonny Doon, California

Dilts, R. and DeLozier, J. (2000) *Encyclopedia of Systemic Neuro-Linguistic Programming and NLP New Coding*, NLP University Press, Scotts Valley, California (Available at http://www.nlpuniversitypress.com/)

Dilts, R. (1983) *Roots Of Neuro-Linguistic Programming*, Meta Publications, Cupertino, California

Dilts, R., Grinder, J., Bandler, R. and DeLozier, J. (1980) *Neuro-Linguistic Programming: Volume 1 The Study of the Structure of Subjective Experience*, Meta Publications, Cupertino, California

Dilts, R.B. and Epstein, T.A. (1995) *Dynamic Learning*, Meta Publications, Capitola

Dilts, R.B. (1994-1995) *Strategies of Genius, Volume I, II, and III*, Meta Publications, Capitola

Dilts, R.B., Epstein, T. and Dilts, R.W. (1991) *Tools for Dreamers*. Capitola, California: Meta Publications

Driscoll, R., Davis, K.E. and Lipetz, M.E. (1972) "Parental Interference and Romantic Love: The Romeo and Juliet Effect" p 1-10 in Journal of Personality and Social Psychology" Number 24, 1972

Engelhard, I.M., van den Hout, M.A., Janssen, W.C. and van der Beek, J., (2010) "Eye movements reduce vividness and emotionality of "flashforwards"" Behaviour Research and Therapy

Erickson, M.H. (1980) *The Collected Papers of Milton H. Erickson Vol I* (ed Rossi, E.L.) Irvington, New York

Erickson, M.H. and Gilligan, S. eds., (2010), *The Legacy of Milton H. Erickson: Selected Papers of Stephen Gilligan, Zeig, Tucker and Theisen*, Phoenix, Arizona

Erickson, M.H. and Rossi, E.L. (1989) *The February Man* Brunner/Mazel, New York

Ericsson, K. A. (2003) "How the expert-performance approach differs from traditional approaches to expertise in sports: In search of a shared theoretical framework for studying expert performance." In J. Starkes and K. A. Ericsson (Eds.) *Expert performance in sport: Recent advances in research on sport expertise.* (pp. 371-401). Champaign, Illinois : Human Kinetics.

Ericsson, K. A. (2003) "The search for general abilities and basic capacities: Theoretical implications from the modifiability and complexity of mechanisms mediating expert performance" In R. J. Sternberg and E. L. Grigorenko (Eds.) *Perspectives on the psychology of abilities, competencies, and expertise.* (pp. 93-125). Cambridge: Cambridge University Press.

Ericsson, K. A. (2004) "Deliberate practice and the acquisition and maintenance of expert performance in medicine and related domains" in *Academic Medicine*. 10, S1-S12.

Fadiga, L., Fogassi, G., Pavesi, G. and Rizzolatti, G. (1995) "Motor Facilitation during action observation: a magnetic stimulation study" p 2608-2611 in Journal of Neurophysiology, No. 73, 1995

Fiedler, F.E. (1951) "Factor analysis of psychoanalytic, non-directive and Adlerian therapeutic relationships" p 32-38 in *Journal of Consulting Psychology*, No. 15, 1951

Freud S., (1953) "Mourning and melancholia". In *The Standard Edition of the Complete Psychological Works of Sigmund Freud, Volume 14* (ed J Strachey): p 239–58. Hogarth Press, 1953

Frewen, P. A., Brown, M. F., Steuwe, C., & Lanius, R. A. (2015). Latent profile analysis and principal axis factoring of the DSM-5 dissociative subtype. *European Journal of Psychotraumatology*

Gardner, H. (1993) *Frames Of Mind: The Theory Of Multiple Intelligences*, BasicBooks, New York, 1993

Genser-Medlitsch, M. and Schütz, P. (1997) "Does Neuro-Linguistic psychotherapy have effect? New Results shown in the extramural section." Vienna: Martina Genser-Medlitsch and Peter Schütz, ÖTZ-NLP,

Goodkin K., Blancy N.T., Feaster D. et alia (1992) "Active coping style is associated with natural killer cell cytotoxicity in asymptomatic HIV-1 seropositive homosexual men" *Journal of Psychosomatic Research* 1992, 36:635-650

Gordon, T. (1995) "Teaching People To Create Therapeutic Environments" in Suhd, M. M. ed *Positive Regard*, Science and Behaviour Books, Palo Alto California, pp 301-336

Gordon, T. (1978) *Leader Effectiveness Training*, Peter H. Wyden, New York

Gordon, T. (1970) *Parent Effectiveness Training*, Peter H. Wyden, New York

Gordon, T. (1974) *Teacher Effectiveness Training*, Peter H. Wyden, New York

Gordon, T. (1989) *Teaching Children Self Discipline At Home And At School*, Random House, New York

Gottman, J.M. and Silver, N. (1999) *The Seven Principles For Making Marriage Work* Three Rivers Press, New York

Gottman, J.M. (1999) *The Marriage Clinic* W.W. Norton and Co., New York, 1999

Gray, R., & Bourke, F. (2015). Remediation of intrusive symptoms of PTSD in fewer than five sessions: A 30- person pre-pilot study of the RTM Protocol. *Journal of Military, Veteran and Family Health*, 1(2), 85-92. doi: doi:10.3138/jmvfh.3119

Gray, R. and Liotta, R. (2012) "PTSD: Extinction, Reconsolidation and the
    Visual-Kinesthetic Dissociation Protocol"
    http://home.comcast.net/~richardmgray/PTSDnVKDprepub.pdf

Grinder, J.; Bostic St. Clair, C. (2002). *Whispering in the Wind*. Scotts
    Valley,CA: J & C. Enterprises.

Gurney, S. (2001) "Gurney's Gossip" Online Edition 2001
    (http://www.perceptionkayaking.com/ctc2001.htm)

Hall, L.M. (2000) "A Few Secrets About Wealth Building" p 25-31 in
    Anchor Point journal, Vol 14, No. 4, April 2000

Hatfield, E., Cacioppo, J. and Rapson, R. (1994) *Emotional Contagion*
    Cambridge University Press, Cambridge, 1994

Howard, J.W. and Dawes, R.M. (1976) "Linear prediction of marital
    happiness" p 478-480 of *Personality and Social Psychology Bulletin*,
    No 2, 1976

Jacobson, S. (1983) *Metacation: Prescriptions For Some Ailing
    Educational Processes*, Meta Publications, Cupertino, California

Jensen, Eric, (1994) *The Learning Brain*, Turning Point for Teachers

Jones, M. Cover (1924) "A Laboratory Study of Fear: The Case Of Peter"
    p 308-315 in *Pedagogical Seminary*, Number 31, 1924

Kasser, T. and Ryan, R.M. (1996) "Further Examining The American
    Dream: Differential Correlates Of Intrinsic And Extrinsic Goals" p
    280-287 in *Personality and Social Psychology Bulletin*, Vol 22, No. 3,
    1996

Kelly, K. (2007) *The Secret Of "The Secret"* Sydney, Australia: Pan
    Macmillan

Kisilevsky, B.S., Hains, S.M.J., Lee, K., Xie, X., Huang, H., Ye, H.-H., et
    al. (2003) "Effects of experience on fetal voice recognition", pg 220-
    224 in *Psychological Science*, No. 14, 2003

Kohn, A. (1996) *Beyond Discipline: From Compliance to Community*,
    Association for Supervision and Curriculum Development,
    Alexandria, Virginia

Kohn, A. (1986) *No Contest: The Case Against Competition*, Houghton
    Mifflin, Boston

Kohn, A. (1993) *Punished By Rewards*, Houghton Mifflin, Boston

Kohn, A. (1990) *The Brighter Side Of Human Nature: Altruism And
    Empathy In Everyday Life* Harper Collins, New York

Lambert, M. and Bergin, A. (1994) "The Effectiveness of Psychotherapy"
    in Bergin, A. and and Garfield, S. *Handbook of Psychotherapy and
    Behaviour Change* Wiley, New York

Langer, E.J. (1989) *Mindfulness*. Reading, Massachusetts: Addison-Wesley

Lee, H. W., Bradburn, J., Johnson, R. E., Lin, S.-H. (J.), & Chang, C.-H.
    (D.). (2019). The benefits of receiving gratitude for helpers: A daily
    investigation of proactive and reactive helping at work. Journal of
    Applied Psychology, 104(2), 197–213.

LeFevre, D.N. (1988) *New Games For The Whole Family* Perigee, New York

Lerner, H.G. (1985) *The Dance of Anger,* Harper & Row, New York

Lieberman, S.A. (1991) *New Traditions: Redefining Celebrations For Today's Family* Noonday Press, New York

Locke, E.A. and Latham, G.P. (1990) "Work Motivation and Satisfaction: Light At The End Of The Tunnel" in *Psychological Science* 1, p 240-246, 1990

MacQueen, G., Marshall, J., Perdue, M. Siegel, S. and Bienenstock, J. (1989) "Pavlovian Conditioning of Rat Mucosal Mast Cells to Secrete Rat Mast Cell Protease II" p 83-85 in *Science*, 6 January 1989

Maruta, M., Colligan, R., Malinchoc, M. and Offord, K. (2000) "Optimists vs. Pessimists: Survival Rate Amongst Medical Patients Over A 30 Year Period" p 140-143 in *Mayo Clinic Proceedings*, Vol 75; Number 2, February 2000

Mavredakis, P. (1989) *Super Speller Strategy*, VHS Video from legacy Home Video, Beverley Hills, California, 1989

Meece, J.L., Wigfield, A. and Eccles, J.S. (1990) "Predictors of Math Anxiety and its Influence on Young Adolescents' Course Enrollment Intentions and Performance in Mathmatics" in *Journal of Educational Psychology* 82, p 60-70

Meltzoff, A. and Moore, K. (1977) "Imitation of Facial and Manual Gestures by Human Neonates" p 75-78 in *Science* magazine, Vol 198, No. 4312, 7 October 1977

Miller, S. D., Hubble, M.A. and Duncan, B.L. (1996) *Handbook of Solution Focused Brief Therapy*, San Francisco: Jossey-Bass

Monterosso, S., Lyubomirsky, K., White, K. and Lehman, D.R. (2002) "Maximising Versus Satisficing: Happiness Is A Matter Of Choice" p 1178-1197 in *Personality and Social Psychology*, No 83 (5), 2002

Muss, D. (1991) "A New Technique For Treating Post-Traumatic Stress Disorder" in British Journal of Clinical Psychology, 30, p 91-92, 1991

Muss, Dr D. (1991) *The Trauma Trap.* Doubleday, London

Nate, S. (2004) "Eye Accessing Cues: A Study in Storage and Retrieving Information" p 35-50 in *Anchor Point*, Volume 18, No 4, June 2004

Nightingale, E. (2009) "The Strangest Secret" published on line at http://www.innovationtools.com/Articles/SuccessDetails.asp

Oettingen, G. (2000) "Expectancy Effects on Behaviour Depend on Self-Regulatory Thought" p 101-129 in *Social Cognition*, No. 18, 2000

Oettingen, G. and Gollwitzer, P.M. (2002) "Self-Regulation of Goal Pursuit: Turning Hope Thoughts into Behaviour" p 304-307 in *Psychological Inquirer*, No 13, 2002

Oettingen, G. and Mayer, D. (2002) "The Motivating Function of Thinking About The Future: Expectations Versus Fantasies" p 1198-1212 in *Journal of Personality and Social Psychology*, No. 83, 2002

Oettingen, G. Pak, H. and Schnetter, K. (2001) "Self-Regulation of Goal Setting: Turning Free Fantasies About the Future Into Binding Goals" p 736-753 in *Journal of Personality and Social Psychology*, No 80, 2001

Ornstein, R., and Sobel, D. (1989) The Healing Brain, MacMillan, London

Paller, K.A. and Vos, J.L., (2004) "Memory reactivation and consolidation during sleep" *Learning & Memory Journal*, 11, p 664-670

Perls, F. (1969) *In And Out Of The Garbage Pail* Real People Press, Lafayette, California

Perls, F.S. (1969) *Gestalt Therapy Verbatim* Real People Press, Moab, Utah

Pham, L.B. and Taylor, S.E. (1999) "From Thought to Action: Effects of Process Versus Outcome Based Mental Simulations on Performance." P 250-260 in *Personality and Social Psychology Bulletin*, No. 25, 1999

PMC4390557. *Try it yourself*: http://traumadissociation.com/pcl5-ptsd

Pogrebin, L.C. (1983) *Family Politics* McGraw-Hill, New York

Pomerantz, E. (2001) "Parent & Child Socialization: Implications for development of depressive syndromes" p 510-525 in *Journal of family Psychology*, Number 15, 2001

Prime Time Productions, (2006) *The Secret DVD*

Prior, R. and O'Connor, J. (2006) *NLP & Relationships* Thorsons, London, 2000-06-28

Prochaska, J.O., Norcross, J.C. and Diclemente, C.C. (1994) *Changing For Good.* New York: William Morrow & Co.

Reckert, H.W. (1994) "Test anxiety… removed by anchoring in just one session?" in *Multimind*, NLP Aktuell, No 6, November/December 1994

Redondo, R.L., Kim, J., Arons, A.L., Ramirez, S. Liu, X. &Tonegawa, S. (2014) "Bidirectional switch of the valence associated with a hippocampal contextual memory engram", *Nature* Volume: 513, Pages: 426–430, 18 September 2014, doi:10.1038/nature13725

Rindfleisch, A., Burroughs, J. and Denton, F. (1997) "Family Structure, Materialism and Compulsive Consumption," p 312-325 in *The Journal of Consumer Research*, Vol 23, No. 4, March 1997

Rizzolatti, G., Fadiga, L., Gallese, V. and Fogassi, L. (1996) "Premotor cortex and the recognition of motor actions" p 131-141 in *Cognitive Brain Research*, No. 3, 1996

Rizzolatti,G. and Arbib, M.A. (1998) "Language within our grasp" p 188-194 in *Trends in Neuroscience*, No. 21, 1998

Robbins, A. (1986) *Unlimited Power*, Fawcett Columbine, New York

Rosenberg, M. (1999) *Nonviolent Communication: A Language of Compassion* Puddle dancer, Del Mar, California

Rossi, E.L. ed, (1989) *The Collected Papers of Milton H. Erickson On Hypnosis, Volume IV,* Irvington, New York

Satir, V. (1967) *Conjoint Family Therapy* Science and Behaviour Books, Palo Alto, California

Satir, V. (1972) *Peoplemaking,* Science and Behaviour, Palo Alto, California

Schacter, D.L. (1996) Searching For Memory Basic Books, New York

Schnurr, P.P., Lunney, C.A., and Sengupta, A. (2004) "Risk Factors for the Development Versus Maintenance of Posttraumatic Stress Disorder", *Journal of Traumatic Stress,* Vol. 17, No. 2, April 2004, pp. 85-95

Schwarz, N., Bless, H., Strack, F., Klumpp, G., Rittenauer-Schatka, H., & Simons, A. (1991). Ease of retrieval as information: Another look at the availability heuristic. *Journal of Personality and Social Psychology,* Vol 61, No. 2, page 195-202

Seligman, (1997) M.E.P. *Learned Optimism* Random House, Milsons Point, Sydney

Seligman, M.E.P. (1995) *The Optimistic Child* Random House, Sydney

Senay, I., Albarracín, D. and Noguchi, K. (2010) "Motivating goal-directed behavior through introspective self-talk: the role of the interrogative form of simple future tense" *Psychological Science* Vol 21, No. 4: p 499-504, April 2010

Shapiro, F., (1995) *Eye Movement Desensitization and Reprocessing,* Guilford Press, New York

Sheets, Connor Adams (2012) "The East European Miracle: How Did Poland Avoid The Global Recession?" *International Business Times,* September 29, 2012

Shoda, Y., Mischel, W. & Peake, P.K. (1990) "Predicting adolescent cognitive and self-regulatory competencies from preschool delay of gratification" Page 978-986 in *Developmental Psychology,* 26 (6), 1990,

Short, D., Erickson, B.A. and Erickson-Klein, R., (2005), *Hope & Resiliency: Understanding the Psychotherapeutic Strategies of Milton H. Erickson,* Crown Publishing, Bancyfelin, United Kingdom

Simons, D.J. and Levin, D.T. (1998) "Failure to detect changes to people during real-world interaction" p 644 in *Psychonomic Bulletin And Review,* Vol. 4, 1998

Slater, P. (1980) *Wealth Addiction.* Dutton, New York

Slavik, D.J. (2003) "Keeping your eyes on the prize : outcome versus process focused social comparisons and counterfactual thinking" Thesis (Ph. D.), Fayetteville: University of Arkansas

Solter, A.J. (1990) *The Aware Baby* Shining Star Press, Goleta, California

Squire, L. R., and Paller, K. A. (2000) "The Biology of Memory", Chapter 3.4 in Williams & Wilkins, Harold I. Kaplan, M.D, Benjamin J.

Sadock, M.D and Virginia A. Sadock, M.D.Kaplan & Sadock's *Comprehensive Textbook of Psychiatry*, Lippincott

Steenkamp, M, Litz, B, W Hoge, C, & Marmar, C. (2015). Psychotherapy for Military-Related PTSD A Review of Randomized Clinical Trials. *JAMA*, 314(15):489-500. Doi:10.1001/JAMA.2015.8370

Swack, J.A., (1992) "A Study of Initial Response and Reversion Rates of Subjects Treated With The Allergy technique", in *Anchor Point*, Vol 6, No2, Feb 1992

Taleb, N.N. (2007) *Fooled By Randomness* Penguin, London, 2007

Thalgott, M.R. (1986) "Anchoring: A "Cure" For Epy" p 347-352 in *Academic Therapy*, Volume 21, No 3, January 1986

Timpany, L. (2005) "Building Outcome Bridges" p 3-4 in *Trancescript* Number 36, October 2005

Tylee, D S., Gray, R, Glatt, S J., & Bourke, F. (2017). Evaluation of the reconsolidation of traumatic memories protocol for the treatment of PTSD: a randomized, wait-list-controlled trial. *Journal of Military, Veteran and Family Health*, 3(1), 21-33. doi: 10.3138/jmvfh.4120.

Van den Berg, D and van der Gaag, E., (2012) "Treating trauma in psychosis with EMDR: A pilot study" *Journal of Behavior Therapy and Experimental Psychiatry*, Volume 43, Issue 1, March 2012, Pages 664-671

Walker, F. and Walker, P. (1987) *Natural Parenting: Practical Guide For fathers and Mothers – Conception to Age 3*, Bloomsbury

Walker, P. (2007) "Young Minds and Emotions" on line at http://www.thebabyswebsite.com/about-the-babys-website.html, 2007

Waltman, S.(2006) http://integrationcoach.wordpress.com/2006/08"Integration Coaching"

Wattles, W. (2006) *The Science of Getting Rich*. Rockford, Illinois: BN Publishing,

Watzlawick, P. (1976) *How Real Is Real* Vintage Books, New York

Weathers, F. W., Huska, J. A., & Keane, T. M. (1991). The PTSD checklist military version (PCL-M). Boston, MA: National Center for PTSD.

Weathers, F. W., Litz, B. T., Herman, D., Huska, J., & Keane, T. (1994). *The PTSD checklist-civilian version (PCL-C)*. Boston, MA: National Center for PTSD.

Weathers, F. W., Litz, B. T., Keane, T. M., Palmieri, P. A., Marx, B. P., & Schnurr, P. P. (2014). PTSD Checklist for DSM-5 (PCL-5). National Center for PTSD. Retrieved June 3, 2015, from http://www.ptsd.va.gov/professional/assessment/adult-sr/ptsd-checklist.asp

Weeks, D., (1994) *The Eight Essential Steps To Conflict Resolution*, G.P. Putnam's Sons, New York

Wegner, D. (1991) "Transactive Memory In Close Relationships" in *Journal of Personality and Social Psychology*, Vol 61, No. 6, p 923-929

Williams, J.H.G., Whiten, A., Suddendorf, T. and Perrett, D.I. (2001) "Imitation, mirror neurons and autism" p 287-295 in *Neuroscience and Biobehavioural Review*, No 25, 2001

Williams, P. and Williams, R. (2003) How To Be Like Women Of Influence, Health Communications Inc, Deerfield Beach, Florida

Wilson, E. (1983) *What Is To Be Done About Violence Against Women* Penguin, Harmonsworth, England

Wilson, G.D., and McLaughlin, C. (2001) *The Science of Love* Fusion Press, London

Wiseman, R. (2009) *59 Seconds: Think A Little, Change A Lot.* London: Macmillan,

Wood, J., Elaine Perunovic, W., & Lee, J. (2009). Positive Self-Statements: Power for Some, Peril for Others. *Psychological Science* Psychological Science July 1, 2009 vol. 20 No. 7, pages 860-866

Yapko, M.D. (1992) *Hypnosis and the Treatment of Depressions*, Brunner/Mazel, New York

Zeigarnik, A.V. (1927) "Über das behalten von erledigten und unerledigten Handlungen" (The retention of completed and uncompleted actions) p 1-85 in *Psychologische Forschung*, No. 9, 1927

Dr Richard Bolstad is a certified trainer with the International NLP Association and five other international training organisations. Richard has a doctorate in clinical hypnotherapy and is a member of the New Zealand Association of Psychotherapists. He is a trained teacher and a registered nurse. His previous book, *Transforming Communication* is a required text in a number of degree level programs, training counsellors, health professionals, teachers, managers and parents. His twelve previous books are published in a number of different languages. He is a parent and grandparent, and lives with his wife Julia Kurusheva north of Auckland, New Zealand. His articles have appeared in numerous journals, and he teaches these skills in Asia, Australasia, the Americas and Europe. More information about his trainings and books is available from The Transformations International internet site at: www.transformations.net.nz. Richard runs trainings in Australasia, Asia and Europe each year. He has over 150 articles published in International magazines, in numerous languages. He is the developer of innovative NLP techniques and models used in business, education and psychotherapy. His book Transforming Communication has been a required text in several New Zealand and Japanese degree programmes, and has been used as the basis for training managers at New Zealand Inland Revenue and several New Zealand corporations and educational institutions. His book RESOLVE, translated into many languages, is the basis of a University paper at the University of Pyatigorsk in Russia (where psychologists are trained for work in the Chechyan war zone). He has also run world service projects such as training Psychiatrists in Sarajevo to deal with Post Traumatic Stress Disorder in survivors of the Bosnian and Kosovo conflicts, and training helpers to cope with the 2011 earthquake in Christchurch, the 2009 tsunami in Samoa and the 2011 tsunami in Japan. **Transformations** is New Zealand's largest NLP training organisation. It runs NLP Practitioner, Master Practitioner and Trainer certification for the International Association for NLP. In New Zealand, its trainings include introductory weekends, 9 day NLP intensives and full 18 day certifications.

"Having worked in the training and communications field for more than 20 years I have experienced a great number of trainers and speakers, but very few great speakers and trainers. Richard Bolstad is one of those great presenters. His absolute credibility is the result of a depth and breadth of knowledge gained internationally and nationally. Richard has an outstanding reputation in his specialist field of communication and NLP. Richard's workshops are practical, immediately applicable and fun to experience for the participants in the workshops. The skills taught will bring benefit to both work and personal lives. If there is one speaker you and your people get to this year make sure it's Richard."- Phillippa Elliot, Past President, New Zealand Association for Training and Development

www.ingramcontent.com/pod-product-compliance
Lightning Source LLC
Chambersburg PA
CBHW070710250726
48662CB00001B/343